THE DUEL

A Spiritual Fight between Immoveable
object (Fundamentalism) and
Irresistible force (Free Will)

by

STEVE BRYAN

authorHOUSE®

AuthorHouse™ UK Ltd.
500 Avebury Boulevard
Central Milton Keynes, MK9 2BE
www.authorhouse.co.uk
Phone: 08001974150

First published by AuthorHouse 23/08/2007

ISBN: 978-1-4259-9322-1 (e)
ISBN: 978-1-4259-9321-4 (sc)

Printed in the United States of America
Bloomington, Indiana

This book is printed on acid-free paper.

Isaiah 58v11

ACKNOWLEDGEMENTS

I read somewhere recently a revised version of the saying, 'behind every successful man there is a woman.' It went something like this 'behind every successful man there is a surprised woman.'

In my case I believe that probably both are true.

When my older daughter Rebekah heard I was writing a book and I was serious she reminded me of the saying 'There is a book inside each of us' and was very encouraging and positive. My younger daughter Naomi asked if the book could be dedicated to her.

In any event thank you to my family, Tricia, Rebekah, Naomi and Jake, who have to live with me and may have a word or two to say to the readers of this book, about how my practice fits in with theory.

A book like this comes about from many years of experience in the world. Over such a long period of time many people play a role in shaping and moulding our view of the world. My parents, brothers and sisters have played a vital role. I'm just sorry that my mum is not around to see this. Mum, thanks for predicting all those years ago so accurately where you thought my gifts and abilities lay.

There is a special thank you to Andy Charles and Linda Grove. Andy, over recent years you have become a close friend and honest critic. Linda you have worked tirelessly to keep track of the many revisions and typing of this manuscript, not an easy task from such a hard taskmaster. Thank you both for believing in this book and for your constant encouragement and support.

And there's my Nephew Jonathan Forrest, a recent graduate in the area of arts and media study. I asked Jonathan to do the artwork for the cover of this book. As a big bonus I discovered that we are very much of like mind. Discussions with you on this book seem to confirm the need to publish this material. Without realising it you were a crucial piece of the jigsaw. Thank you.

My final thanks go to John Smith. I asked John to do a last minute proof read and his input brought to light some remaining punctuation and grammatical errors and also encouraged me to re-order the final chapters. Naturally, all remaining errors are my own.

CONTENTS

PREFACE

Perhaps from the birth of Humanity one thing has evaded mankind, lasting peace. Real lasting worldwide peace has seemed like the illusive 'Scarlet Pimpernel'. People and nations from all times have sought it here, there and everywhere, perhaps even caught up with it at times, only to discover it evaporating right in front of their eyes.

Any sort of peace achieved has been full of uncertainty and suspicion. Here we are in the 21st Century with generations of scientific achievement and education under our belt but still real lasting peace appears outside our grasp.

The whole world is like a very dry tinderbox waiting to go up in smoke. Outbreaks of fire spring up almost at random in different areas of the planet and governments of the world rush to put them out. Ironically in the dash to do so, they seem to generate more fuel for uncertainty, tension and war.

On the front page of the Independent newspaper on the 17 January 2007, an article by Robert Cornwall revealed that the Doomsday Clock would be moved forward for the first time in five years, indicating that the world was at its most unstable in its history. For 60 years it had depicted how close the world was to nuclear disaster and scientists moved its hands forward to show that we are facing the gravest threat in 20 years.

If the general question is asked "What causes war?" I suspect the average man and woman in the street would say religion and politics. In some respects I concur with this, as does history.

Religion and politics have served to galvanise people into groups. Warring factions that believe their point of view must prevail over all others.

Although large numbers of people choose the groups they belong to, this is not true for the majority. For most people what group we belong to is chosen for us. Many factors play a part, but by far the biggest factor for this placement into a group, is where we are born.

In itself, the group we belong to is not the problem directly, but it is the attitude, the control and the effect the group has on its members that is the problem.

The solution I believe is easy! It is the subject of this book.

Ironically, we will never find peace. Peace will find us. More precisely it is already on the way. It is for this very reason that we may think that peace is further from our grasp than ever before. Take heart it is coming and cannot be stopped.

Transition always causes major upheaval. If you have ever had an extension built onto your house you will know just how this feels. Before the work starts the house is often ok and inhabitable but you decide to make it better for the future. The plans are drawn up, approval granted and then the work begins. No matter how well prepared you are the messy transition period tempts you often to wish you had left things as they were. The only thing that keeps you moving forward is the knowledge that you can't go back and that things will be better when the work is finished.

From the time of Christ up until the turn of the Century we have been living in the era of Pisces. This era is characterised by group dominance. The average person is not capable of thinking for himself and must be told what to do.

With the heralding in, around the start of the new century, a new era, the era of Aquarius began. This era is characterised by people understanding truth and thinking for themselves.

The transition period is causing great upheavals in the groups. Religious and political groups that have dominated are not exempt.

In this generation we have seen from a political group point of view, the changes that have taken place in Eastern Europe. The fall of the Berlin wall and a move away from communism.

By nature mankind does not like change. Even when change benefits it is resisted. We like the way things have always been done. It is not uncommon for people to talk about the 'good old days' when generally speaking most changes benefit mankind.

When change is necessary it is better accepted in small increments than all at once. It would be true to say that radical change thrust upon the human frame, especially those that challenge our cultural way of life, our emotions and thinking, would destroy us.

The change from Pisces to Aquarius began at least half a century ago. Historically we see it in examples like the changes that Martin Luther King started when he changed how the world viewed different coloured races.

Change is facilitated if it is presented by someone within the group rather than an outsider. Such individuals, however, run the risk of being branded as traitors and/or 'turncoats'. In religious and political groups all over the world this transition has begun.

Up until now group dominance has acted like dams, sealing in their followers. A crack has appeared, small amounts of water have leaked out. No amount of desperate measures to contain this leakage by group dominance can prevent the trickle from becoming a flow and the flow from becoming an outpouring flood and deluge.

The question may be asked, "If a relatively small number of dominant groups could not achieve peace amongst themselves won't the job become totally impossible when every individual wins the right to free thinking and expression?" On the contrary peace cannot be imposed on people or nations. It is only as people become free in themselves that they can discover real peace.

> *"Then you will know the truth, and the truth will set you free" John 8v32*

The world will never find peace if it is looked for where it is not to be found. Jesus breathed on disciples and gave them peace, a peace that was beyond all human comprehension. He left that peace for all mankind. In becoming like him we embrace that peace for ourselves and the whole of mankind. This is the only future for mankind.

THE DUEL

INTRODUCTION

Like any author giving birth to a new book, I have read, edited, re-read and re-edited the material many times over.

A question that keeps coming to mind is why the title *The Duel*. To answer the question simply and honestly, these were the words going around in my head the morning I woke knowing I had a book to write. A host of other titles would have been appropriate for this work; examples I have considered are:

1. What Fundamental Error does the Church and the State Constantly Make?
2. How to Break Free from the Opinions of Others
3. Discovering your True Identity and Purpose in Life
4. How a Terrorist is made.

Strange as it may seem at first glance, this little book is about all the things mentioned above. Naturally not every book will appeal to everyone, but I am confident that if you are an earnest seeker of truth and have unanswered questions that over time you have put on the 'back burner' of life, but are questions that keep on flaring up from time to time to trouble you, this book is certainly for you.

The Duel is about a conflict, a fight, primarily between two schools of thinking. In this book, the two schools are 'Traditional Thinking' and 'Original Thinking'. 'Traditional Thinking' is based on history, the popular accepted viewpoint of the day, on dogma and fundamentalism. 'Original Thinking' is simply to think outside the box of history, to question the popular, dogmatic accepted view of the day and fundamentalism. In everybody's life there will come occasions when these two views will clash. These significant times in our experience are what I have called *The Duel*. At these crossroad points in our experience, we must fight. The outcome will determine whether we advance in our life, merely mark time or (worse still), go backwards.

You can experience this *Duel* at almost any time you like. Simply find a question that has never been fully answered to your personal satisfaction, now begin again to seek the answer. Make it a diligent search in which you will promise to be totally open and honest with your heart and conscience. Does your honest search lead you outside the box of Traditional and Popular Thinking? Does it call into question accepted dogma and the fundamentalist viewpoint? If it does, at this point *The Duel* begins. Your Original Thinking and search will be met with opposition. Press on and the objection will become ridicule. Press yet further, following your heart and conscience, and the ridicule will turn to hostility. Like any *duel*, there comes a final showdown where one view must die to give full acceptance to the other. Choose wisely my friend, the outcome of eternity is bound up in the answer. Only stop your search for truth when every 'i' is dotted and every 't' is crossed to your total satisfaction.

Honesty with yourself is the answer you are seeking.

Very often if you look closely enough, you will see that those that give way to Traditional and Popular Thinking preferring to stick to the fundamentalist viewpoint, often work in the realm of theory. Those who are at home with Original Thinking, work in the realm of reality. They need to see it and experience it for themselves. ***The Duel*** therefore is not only Traditional and Popular Thinking versus Original Thinking, but also a choice between theory and practice.

This book is primarily aimed at all those who go to Church and would consider themselves Christians and hence I have quoted the Bible as the main reference. Secondly, those who used to go to Church, but no longer attend should read this book. Thirdly, those that do not go to Church, but maybe cannot quite put their finger on why they do not attend should read it. Finally, those who oppose the Church and what it represents should read it.

In short, I think everyone should read *'**The Duel**'*.

A MESSAGE TO YOU

Dear Reader

It is almost certain that I may never meet you in person, but I regard you as my brother/sister and certainly a friend. Whatever you may feel or think of what is written in these pages, that relationship will never alter.

At first reading, what I have to say may seem like liberal thinking *Judges 17:6 "everyone did as he saw fit"* or the introduction of some new theology. Nothing could be further from the truth.

No trace of liberalness is to be found in these pages – on the contrary, the practices here are rooted in discipline, self-control and determination on the part of each and every person on the planet, as we move individually and collectively back to God.

Our actions must always be with careful concern as to how, what we do, will impact on others on our planet, and indeed even on the whole Universe. This thought is at the very core of this book *'No man is an island'*[1].

This is certainly no attempt to introduce new theology whether blatantly or in disguise. In fact, it seeks not to disagree with any point you may consider important to you. I have no desire or wish to move you from your views, or beliefs you hold most true and dear!

This generation has come to the place where it will not be dictated to or manipulated by others. Once the Church had all the power, today that power ebbs away, people find it out of touch and irrelevant. When the Church speaks on issues of the day, people often treat what it has to say with outward disdain.

The same is true of Politics. People seem more eager to vote in a reality TV programme, and certainly with more enthusiasm, than they are interested in voting for a politician. There is a new fervour on the part of the leaders of religious organisations and political parties to wake the nations' interest in both the Church and Politics respectively– why are they having to do this? Before you read on, answer the question for yourself as honestly as you can, then compare your answer with mine.

No cheating please!

******** *please stop now and do this exercise* ********

Both Church and Politicians come across as insincere! Their rhetoric says one thing, but their actions say another, both talk about serving but both appear eager for the power. Therefore over a period of time the people have become disillusioned and discouraged. They have simply lost interest. I believe that if you dig down through the layers, it will be found that fear and self-interest are the driving force of both Church and State. (To a small degree we will explore this in these pages – but really it is worthy of a book in its own right).

Both Church and State are eager to warn of the dangers of neglect in their particular area of interest. Ironically they both speak the truth in some respect, but unwittingly constitute significantly to the problem of apathy and disinterest.

Jesus said a similar thing in His day.

> *"The teachers of the law (the Scribes) and the Pharisees sit in Moses' seat. So you must obey them and do everything they tell you. But do not do what they do for they do not practise what they preach." Matthew 23v2-3*

> *"For I tell you that unless your righteousness surpasses that of the Pharisees and the teachers of the law, you will certainly not enter the Kingdom of Heaven" Matthew 5v20*

It is time for both these parties to wake up to this truth. The parallels between the Church and State seem obvious to me, but my purpose here is to speak primarily about the Church.

CHAPTER 1

YOU ARE TOTALLY UNIQUE

Very recently the Baptist Union of Great Britain in conjunction with the Baptist World Centenary Congress held an International Music concert at Symphony Hall in Birmingham. The concert was a celebration of diverse expressions of Christian worship from around the world. Well, I have to tell you this, I was moved to the heights of Heaven as I listened to the artists' performances, even as I pen this, a tingling sensation is running through my body.

The programme was over two hours, comprising a variety of diverse artists (soloists, small groups, choirs and an ensemble of over 120 young people). Two of the performances brought the roof down with repeated standing ovations, the atmosphere was electric. The first of these exceptional performances was a Korean children and adult choir, led by Reverend Tom Song[(1)].

The second talented performance of outstanding quality was an artist by the name of Larnelle Harris[(2)]. His ability was simply 'off the planet' scale of brilliance. I have never heard someone do so much with his voice. Without a doubt, I did not want it to end. I'm guessing the majority of people in the Concert Hall felt the same way. Very impressive. If you ever get the opportunity to hear him, do not miss it.

As I mentioned earlier there were many times during the concert that I felt a warm tingling sensation passing through me. This sort of feeling happens to many people when we are touched at a very deep soul level involving our entire being. This sensation can be triggered in us by people using the abilities and talents they have refined to a high degree of perfection. There need not be any noticeable religious connection for this feeling to be triggered in people. I am careful to say there need be no religious connection, but I would suggest there is always a spiritual connection, whether this is acknowledged or not.

I personally have been equally affected in this 'spiritual' way by many diverse people and situations. When the England Rugby squad won the World Series, the welcome home scene had the same effect – I was only watching on television and not directly in the atmosphere of the airport or procession through the streets – yet I felt the electricity pulsing through me and was moved almost to tears of joy.

Many musical artists have the same effect on me, such as Elvis Presley, G4, The 3 Tenors. King George II was so moved by hearing the Hallelujah Chorus from Handel's Messiah, that he stood to his feet.

Every man, woman and child on this planet has a gift, a talent, that when refined and used will have an 'electric effect' on the people around them. God gives talents to everyone, regardless of the labels *we* attach to them. That label may be race, colour, sex and even religion. God sees no such labelling.

"For God's gifts and his call are irrevocable" Romans 11v29

We all have talents and abilities that are given to us as gifts, however if they are to impact on the world we will more often than not need to refine them.

This is exactly what Jesus meant when he spoke of the parable of the talents. *Matthew 13v1-23*

When someone offers their refined talents it blesses everyone in the vicinity. Each artist at this concert added a unique contribution. No two acts were the same, yet all without exception expressed worship and praise to God.

God is so great that every bit of creation is a reflection of his magnitude. Using nature as a good yardstick we see sameness and uniqueness everywhere we look. No two snowflakes are identical, no two fingerprints are identical. Thousands upon thousands of species of animals and plants bear witness to this diverse omnipresence of God. Anything or anyone, be it Church or State that seeks to bring us into 'conformity' and 'sameness' works against the unlimited resources of God. Acts of enforced conformability have their roots in self-centeredness. Our creative image is not that of man but of God who is Himself infinity in motion.

A friend of mine was once relating a conversation he had with his local M.P. My friend was expressing a viewpoint different to that of the M.P. and argued his case well. To defend his position, the M.P. accused my friend of "not knowing what he was talking about." This is a phrase, which I hear being repeated more and more often by one or both parties engaged in passionate discussion. In effect the M.P. tried to belittle my friend and tried to rob him of his self-respect.

When people attempt to stifle your unique talents or attempt to belittle you, step back for a moment, listen to the sincere prompting of your heart. Take a moment to regain an understanding of your talents and abilities. Be confident in knowing that you are made in the image of God and your viewpoint is as important as the next person's. Having considered this, then move fearlessly forward.

This understanding of uniqueness cannot be overstated. Just recently I was reminded of this fact from an unexpected place. I was watching for the second time on DVD the movie of 'I Robot' starring Will Smith.[3] The film centres around Will Smith and one very special robot. What they both have in common is their uniqueness. Now I know its only a film, but I believe it was a successful film, at least in part, because it appealed to the uniqueness in us all.

Chapter 2

The Journey

Every life is unique and a personal exciting voyage of discovery. 'You are as unique as the person next to you'. On any voyage of discovery there will be times when you journey with others and times when you must journey alone.

> *"There is a time for everything, and a season for every activity under heaven ..." Ecclesiastes 3v1-8*

If we try to avoid the parts of the journey that we need to do alone, we will never experience the total magic of life.

When we avoid these moments of solitary[1] journeying we miss out on what is truly unique for us.

This solitude is often missed and/or avoided for one of two reasons namely:

1. We find our own company uncomfortable
2. Others wittingly or unwittingly hold us back

Both of these reasons bring us to *The Duel*. In each case we battle either with ourselves or with others.

Other people feel uneasy if you choose to make any part of the journey alone. At best it seems to instil in them a concern for your safety, at worst the feeling that you cannot possibly manage alone.

It is the course of human nature to have others fall into line with our perceived way of thinking and doing. At first reading, this may seem rather over the top, but is it? Ask yourself, how do you react when other people do simple things differently from you?

Examples may be:

How food is prepared

How we squeeze a tube of toothpaste

How we leave the bathroom

You can almost add anything to the list. At best, these differences cause minor irritation to us and we like to 'perfect' these bad habits we see in others. These differences may on one hand keep us away from those that have this effect on us, and at the other extreme they cause us to fall out, argue, fight and even kill. If you are prepared to go along with conforming to other people's expectations, there never is a conflict and therefore, no duel to fight.

From a Spiritual point of view, if we are happy to accept what tradition and popular thinking teaches, there is no duel to fight. We do not challenge its authority or history and therefore, all is well. No-one picks a fight with himself. The Bible states in *Matthew 12v25*, '...*every city or household divided against itself will not stand*'. If you are happy with tradition and popular thought, then these two are perfectly happy with you.

The path I am fully authorised and qualified to describe is the one that is opened up by the Christian faith. However, you can apply whatever I have to say to any of the mainstream faiths (and probably the minor ones also) and you will arrive at the same place.

I have been privileged to have had the benefit of the writings of what I believe to be authoritative figures from other faiths, who have made the same journey I have made; they have had to fight what from their perspective is the same duel, to arrive at the ultimate truth. This is hardly surprising, as the followers of each major faith claim that the way laid out in their religious teachings is the only way.

I say followers of the faith make these claims. The authors themselves do not make such claims, in fact, they really warn against such a course of action. Those of you who are walking the traditional path of Christianity will no doubt wish to quote that Jesus Himself said words like:

> *"...I am the way, and the truth and the life.   No-one comes to the Father except through me ... " John 14v6*

Bear with me, as we open up the way, all I hope will become crystal clear.

Let me say, here and now for the record, that those who follow the Christian teachings need not disregard any of its instructions. Like Christ Himself, I would declare the task at hand is not to destroy the law, but to fulfil it. *Matthew 5v7*

The Church is like a school, instructing men and women in the teachings of Christ and points the way to salvation. All that enter its gates are embarking on a noble road to truth and should expect to graduate with honours – what's the problem then? Why the need for duelling if we follow the Church's tradition and popular teaching? Somewhere along the way, the Church limits the growth of individuals when its personal view is challenged or rejected! Begin to think outside its recommended and traditional boundaries and you will be expected to conform or be disciplined in some way. Discipline can take the form of threats at one end of the scale, right through to excommunication at the other.

For those familiar with the life and times of Christ, you will observe He kept His greatest condemnation and criticism for the established Church. He accused them of blocking the way of earnest seekers, putting great weights of guilt and law keeping on their backs, and worse than that, accused them of making converts *'twice as much a son of hell as you are'. Matthew 23v15.* Jesus duelled with tradition and popular theology of His day and was seemingly killed in **The Duel** at the cross.

What was His crime? He invited people to be honest with themselves, and to dare to think outside the box. He upset the traditional and popular thinking of His day. I say Jesus appeared to lose **The Duel**, but we know that He rose from the dead, triumphing over sin, hypocrisy and death, leading many sons and daughters to the now of eternity.

If you come to **The Duel**, as far as the traditional standpoint is concerned, you will be defeated and dealt a fatal blow. From the point of truth and reality, you will arrive home safe and free. Rest assured, you cannot lose. This truth is already gaining strength all over the world. Just like in the days of Jesus, the poor, the needy, the sick will receive this truth and move on triumphant. Making the claim of Christ just as relevant today as it was 2000 years ago:

> *"But many who are first will be last, and the last first"*
> Mark 10v31

I have no doubt that this book may draw heavy and harsh criticism from the traditional, historical popular view of truth. I may be venomously slandered and criticised, many will be warned to keep away. But that is the nature of **The Duel**. To those who would oppose,

I would ask this simple question in genuine love. What is there to be afraid of?

If you, as mentors and teachers of the traditional Christian doctrine have taught your flock well and have led them to Christ and they know the truth, surely they will dismiss a lie easily.

Elijah mocked the God of Baal,

> *"Shout louder!" he said. "Surely he is a god! Perhaps he is deep in thought, or busy, or travelling. Maybe he is sleeping and must be awakened." 1 Kings 18v27*

Elijah knew that God could speak for Himself and answer for Himself. Truth is truth, it is not changed by what you, I or anyone's point of view might be.

> *Truth will prove itself to be truth. Steve Bryan*

Allow your children to grow up properly, in the image of God to fulfil their calling and journey on the royal route back to God.

> *"Woe to you, teachers of the law and Pharisees, you hypocrites! You shut the kingdom of heaven in men's faces. You yourselves do not enter, nor will you let those enter who are trying to." Matthew 23v13-27*

What is it to be for you dear reader?

CHAPTER 3

MY JOURNEY

I thought it may be helpful if I outlined some of my story so far, highlighting moments when I had to duel and make choices as to whether to stay within the confines of traditional thinking or step out, following my heart.

I am very grateful for my roots. From the age of 0 I was steeped in Church life. At 11 years of age I made a commitment to give my life to Christ. In Church terminology, this is when I became 'born again' – I was baptised (i.e., the full emersion type) 2 years later.

I remember coming home many Sunday evenings and after supper, practising preaching in my room, calling people to commit their lives to Christ. I belonged to the Pentecostal/Evangelical wing of the Christian Church and therefore, supernatural gifts and fervent Evangelism was an important part of my makeup and experience.

At 18 I went off to Kent University to study Biochemistry. The most memorable lectures were given by the Thermodynamics lecturer. Here, this very gifted lecturer taught us how to learn, *"find someone who can explain it in a way you can understand"*. I wish I could remember his name! I sensed he really cared about how we progressed as students. He took the time to explain that no-one could teach us at this level.

To progress we had to have the desire and will to move ahead. If I remember correctly, he also made quantum physics come alive. Little did I know how much these lectures would help me many years later in duel situations, to make choices wisely.

Many times I wrote in my notes words like 'praise the Lord' as I saw many connections between scientific discovery and what I had been brought up to believe as a Christian (brought up to believe – what a telling phrase!).

For the first time I began to realise that the gap between Church and science was not as unbridgeable as I was led to believe, in fact, I saw no major contradiction between science and Biblical teaching. (It seems to me that many areas of science are opening up a path to faith and belief in 'God' far quicker than religion).

In those University years, I attended a FIEC Church (Fellowship of Independent Evangelical Churches), another branch of the main Christian Church; their emphasis was on preaching and evangelism. Compared to my Pentecostal upbringing, there were certainly points of doctrine that they fundamentally disagreed with. The main one that springs to mind was the gifts of the Holy Spirit and their relevance for today.

Within mainstream Christian belief, certain points seem to be central to them all:

    (i)   Creation rather than evolution

    (ii)   Fall of man into sin

    (iii)   Redemption by Christ alone

    (iv)   Heaven to be gained and Hell to be avoided

However, even on these major issues, points of interpretation and descriptions differ immensely. The emphasis produced different practical results in the members, e.g., those that major in 'Gifts of the Holy Spirit' seem to have a more light hearted approach to life, but seem to struggle when crises occur. Groups that play down references to the 'Gifts of the Holy Spirit' and concentrate more on a 'sound teaching' approach, seem to produce a more 'serious minded Christian' better able to cope with the downsides of life.

It seemed to me the different groups within the Christian faith, were about solving a jigsaw puzzle in which the outer edge of the picture was in place, but the details were still unclear. Bits of the pieces were being forced to fit to give desired results. If one piece of the jigsaw is in the wrong place, it means that at least two pieces must be wrong and would mean that the puzzle would never be completed properly.

What I was seeing, witnessing and experiencing was that within mainstream Christianity, many groups had sprung up and become established because they disagreed on what they considered important issues. At the time of writing, the Church of England is at a crossroads with divisions threatened over issues of homosexuality and women ordination. The apostle Paul used anomalies like this, effectively setting one group against another to his advantage. *Acts 23v6-8.*

When I stood back from all of this, which was very confusing to say the least, I promised myself not to take any side, but rather I would be patient to get the answer for myself. *I would hold an open mind until I was totally satisfied* with unswerving conviction. I worked on the premise that a loving God would not want to leave me in a fog of uncertainty.

This particular experience of how different groups of Christians emphasised different doctrines, was resolved for me when I considered the *'parable of the sower' Matthew 13v1-23,* it suddenly became clear that the type of Christian produced depended upon which type of soil he/she was planted in.

From experience, an amazing truth began to dawn on my consciousness. God would bring into my life in a way that we would call coincidental, that which would lead me to answers. Always events would work together, to bring about conviction and certainty to a question I was seeking the answer to. If I was not sure that one of these 'coincidences' was the answer, I never needed to fear, more evidence was brought into my conscious realm.

The story of Gideon springs to mind. In asking for a sign from God that he should lead the people, he put down a fleece and asked it to be wet in the morning, but the ground around it to be dry. The following day his request was granted. An astute person like Gideon realised his answer may have been flawed – the fleece would naturally retain moisture longer than the ground around it! So he asked for the reverse sign as confirmation! God willingly obliged. *Judges 6v36-40*. The laws of physics were suspended in the second test. God is like this always, if we are genuinely unsure, God will work in such a way to help our faith to grow actively.

Truth is truth. Opinion never changes truth. God's truth can withstand any scrutiny over any period of time.

To Him be honour, glory and praise, for ever Amen.

Over the years, I have asked questions of God, if an uncertainty remains I have been honest to say so, with time as the jigsaw comes together, the picture becomes clearer. The fog clears and lifts to reveal the glorious splendour of God. Hearsay, whether right or wrong, simply is no substitute for experiencing reality. Let someone who has explored the heights of space or the depth of the ocean describe what they have seen and experienced. Be moved by their enthusiasm and passion, but if you want to know for yourself, you have to go and experience for yourself. To do otherwise is like listening to someone describe a fantastic meal they have enjoyed. Your taste buds may react, a picture in the mind may be invoked, but you will remain hungry if you do not taste and eat yourself.

So the Bible clearly states:

> '*..taste and see that the Lord is good.' Psalm 34v8.*

> '*but whoever drinks the water I give him will never thirst. Indeed, the water I give him will become in him a spring of water welling up to eternal life. John 4v14*

So many people settle for hearsay and stop short of the experience for themselves – first hand. If we drink at the fountain, out of our inner most beings flow rivers of living water and we will never thirst again.

Are you thirsty? Then go on searching and do not stop until you are satisfied. Drink deep and long, your needs will be fully met. All who come to Christ will be satisfied.

After finishing University in 1977, I became an avid reader in search of truth. I was interested at that time particularly, in the gift of healing. Could the reported miracles Jesus did in His life on earth be repeated again today in my lifetime, or was this department moved from the Church to the advances made in medicine. Jesus Himself declared

> "*I tell you the truth, anyone who has faith in me will do what I have been doing. He will do even greater things than these, because I am going to the Father." John 14v12*

I was fascinated by the stories of many people like Kathryn Kuhlman[1] and Smith Wigglesworth[2], but equally confounded by the lack of hard evidence in my own experience. People seemed to me to be confused between wishful thinking and faith, with many claims and counter claims, with the increase in alternative medicine the picture was very confusing.

Somewhere in this search, interest shifted from healing to a deep desire to 'experience' God. 'Experience' may seem like a strange word, particularly as I have, from the age of 10 claimed to be 'born again' and had the Spirit of God dwelling in me. Anomalies and developing behavioural attitudes in my life deepened the need for real experience. I could identify one hundred percent with the words of Paul.

'I do not understand what I do. For what I want to do I do not do, but what I hate I do.' Romans 7v14

The more I searched the deeper the fog appeared to become!

This stage lasted many years. Looking back, I realise this was a very important – not to be missed experience. In my readings, I came across the works of St John of the Cross, who described this type of experience as the 'Dark night of the Soul'[3].

Reading was a key part for me, one book seemed to lead me to another, then another, then another, in what appeared to be a completely logical and coherent fashion. This stepping from book to book, led me to authors that from a traditional Christian stand point, may have been thought inappropriate. (To this day, I keep my most precious books off my library shelves, away from prying eyes). But I had made a crucial decision, I wanted to know truth for myself first hand, and I promised myself I would follow the trail, wherever it took me.

I trusted that in an earnest desire to know the truth, God would protect me. I was not afraid to let the 'chips fall where they would'. Although walking in a fog, every step was a joy; I found I was not alone. Many had walked this road in every generation and what's more, were walking it with me now.

Elijah at one time thought he was the only one going along the road with God (*1 Kings 19v10*) until he is told that over seven thousand other people were on a similar journey as himself (*1 Kings 19v18*).

Of more recent years the seeking has led me down roads I know I would never have experienced had I stayed within the confines of expected popular thinking and dogma. It has been an experience of ever increasing joy, happiness and contentment. And what's more the journey continues.

Chapter 4

Is the Journey Fraught
with Dangers?

Yes it is! In a very real sense the journey is like walking a tightrope with no knowledge of a safety net to catch you if you fall.

> *"But small is the gate and narrow the road that leads to life, and only a few find it." Matthew 7:14*

On the surface, these may not seem like encouraging statistics, winning the lottery may seem better odds! But rest assured all that firmly, earnestly seek, will find.

> *"Ask, and it will be given to you; seek, and you will find; knock and the door will be opened to you." Matthew 7v7*

The only real danger is stopping and turning back along the way. Jesus says:

> *"No-one who puts his hand to the plough and looks back*
> *is fit for service in the kingdom of God." Luke 9v62*

We need to run the straight race with all our might. Take courage, even if you are 'out of shape' but are determined to arrive, you will. God will assist you at every step along the way. All who start and want to complete the journey back to God will arrive. No question or doubt in my mind. Even if you are distracted, make mistakes, slip up, stop for a while, be courageous, you will arrive if you want to.

The whole of creation will arrange circumstances in your life to make absolutely sure you complete the journey.

> *"...being confident of this, that he who began a good*
> *work in you will carry it on to completion until the day*
> *of Christ Jesus." Philippians 1v6*

To enter the race through the stadium of the established Church is a very useful gateway, but, and this is extremely important, that same gateway that you enter by also has the potential to become your greatest stumbling block!

<u>Deception - the Biggest Issue</u>

No-one on the journey back to God can avoid the process of <u>possible</u> deception. This is a classic catch 22-type scenario. It is a two edged sword that has to be dealt with and overcome. The old saying that there is safety in numbers is very true. Proverbs state that with many heads lies wisdom. Other scriptures indicate that only a fool ignores the advice of others.

The established Church will quote many such scriptures to deter any would-be 'rebel' who would raise questions that challenge tradition and dogma. On one hand our pulpits are filled with preachers, declaring that we should follow Christ, listen for His voice then obey, however, if our listening appears to contradict tradition and dogma, we are pushed back into the box of dogma and accepted belief. There is not a single person chasing after God, who will not be deterred by well meaning instructors to abandon the call they will feel deep within their heart.

<u>How can we navigate this double-sided sword, without inflicting a fatal wound?</u>

Make no mistake, there are some who believe they hear the call of God to go in a certain direction, but are simply deceived. Only recently, radical individuals carried out the London bombings of July 7, 2005. No way can their acts be judged *'with the blessing of God'* – we shall return to this later in the chapter.

Listed below are some of the characteristics a person following the voice of God should look for. If these are present they can move forward with confidence.

They display the fruit of the Spirit – *Galatians 5v22-23*

    (i)   They will wait for as many confirmational signs before moving forward as is necessary to convince.

    (ii)   They are not being pushed by others.

    (iii)   They are willing not to force their views on others.

    (iv)   Their desire will not go away.

Even when all these characteristics are noticed and in evidence, many will still try to deter them from moving forward.

<u>This is the only way forward but you are not alone</u>

Read the life story of any 'Man of God'. Pick any great leader from the Word of God and you will see that they all had to step out alone to obey God, rather than man. *Acts 4v19.* They all had, at some point in their personal growth, to step outside the well-established box of thinking. We have no greater example than the life of Jesus Himself. The established Church obstructed Him at every turn. They accused Him of being a 'Child of the Devil.' *Matthew 12v24*. Despite all the wonderful things He did in the way of miracles, healings and loving people – the established Church executed Him rather than let their principles of tradition and dogma be contradicted.

The question may occur to you 'Why is it necessary to think outside the box?' The answer is really quite simple. No progress can be made if we don't. Think about it, if we settle for what is historically known, how can we ever move forward? How can we evolve if we don't think new thoughts and explore uncharted areas?

In a recent article in the "if" Toyota magazine[1] there was an interesting article about new innovations. In the article they list 10 innovations that are changing the world. Several fascinating quotes are mentioned:

> *"Thinking out of the box is a way of life at Toyota; But it's more difficult than it looks."*

> *"Inventions reached their limit long ago… I see no hope for further development" Julius Frontinus, 1ˢᵗ Century A.D.*

Almost by definition stepping outside the box belongs to the minority, and yet I have mentioned that there is safety to be found in numbers. This is part of the fine line we must walk; are all lemmings doing the right thing?

Earlier in the chapter I mentioned that the established Church was a very useful gateway to enter on our quest, but that it also had the potential to become our greatest stumbling block.

It presents two large stumbling blocks:

1.   Indoctrinates rather than makes disciples

2.   Suppresses free thinking and free will

Christ's command is to make disciples *(Matthew 28v19)* – mature men and women that have learned how to hear and act on the word He speaks to their hearts. Although to a large degree the Church does this, it also indoctrinates its members to believe the collective group understanding. This in itself leads to a stifling of freethinking and free will. This is particularly noticed in what is often referred to as 'Cults'. The techniques used by such groups border on brainwashing its members and removal of freedom until they conform. Literally members are watched and held within the boundaries of the community until the leaders are sure they have totally embraced its teachings, methods and practices.

Although most Churches do not resort to such radical techniques, most will allow freethinking and expression up to a certain point. Any considered serious deviation is met with 'spiritual threats' like, 'you are damming your soul' or 'backsliding.' God never acts in any way against our free will. If we understood this principle of God we would have a good explanation for why things happen within the world that we question a loving God would allow.

Leadership needs to be God like. Challenge individuals by all means if error or deception is suspected. Desire for the well-being of all, but allow a person to follow their heart. Offer guidance with gentleness and be ready to welcome back any that may have strayed into error.

Deception is a double-edged sword, because change whether for the good or bad takes place over a period of time. It is unusual for anyone to be deceived in a moment of time! The path to truth is long and seemingly complex. Moving towards truth (or error) is done by taking a little step at a time, even extreme cults that take over individuals 'brainwash' their students over a period of time.

Human nature cannot generally accept sudden change. To do so could cause injury to the personality. Jesus commented to his disciples:

> *"O unbelieving and perverse generation. How long shall I stay with you? How long shall I put up with you?" Matthew 17v17*

Because change is slow, it can be likened to drifting without realising you may have moved a long way from the shore.

Are we drifting towards or away from God?

CHAPTER 5

KEY CUTTING AND CHINESE WHISPERS. GOING TO THE SOURCE

Recently I had difficulty getting my door key to work in the lock of the main outside door to my office. After a few minutes of twisting, rocking, removing and re-inserting the key I got the lock to eventually open.

At a later time I mentioned this to my good friend Andy who, as part of his job, runs a key cutting service.

He at once told me a possible reason why I had problems with the key. Apparently after a key has been used many times in a lock little bits of the metal can flake off and accumulate in the lock. The technical term for this I am told is 'balling.' In addition to this, dust builds up in the lock. If 'balling' is not too severe the lock can be cleaned out by running graphite, (using a pencil is ideal) along the edges of the key then sliding the key into the lock. The process may need repeating a number of times before it is successful.

This all sounded rather complex and technical to me so I simply asked if he would cut me another key. Before committing to say yes to my request, Andy asked me if the key I had was the original. When I said it was not he was reluctant to cut a key from the copy.

Every time a copy of a key is made there is **always** an error produced. However good the copy, it is never 100% the same as the original, so if a number of new keys are cut from the latest copy there will come a time when the key produced differs significantly from the original so that it simply will not work. Andy always gives the advice to his customers after cutting a new key *'try it before you commit to it'*.

When I heard this information from Andy the parallels between key cutting and the heart of this book *'The Duel'* just seem to come together in my mind like a lock and key.

Chinese Whispers

Each generation is probably familiar with Chinese whispers. Chinese whispers is where a short phrase is passed by word of mouth down a line of people. How the message is received at the end of the line is then compared with the original phrase.

If the game is played properly, with no deliberate attempt to change what is said by any of the participants, the message usually emerges at the end of the line slightly altered from the original. My favourite is where a General at the front line of fighting sends a message through the supply chain back to headquarters as *'send reinforcements we are going to advance.'* The message received at the other end came out as *'send three and four pence we are going to a dance.'*

A minister of a Church once lamented to me that most of his congregation needed to be what he termed *'spoon fed.'* No matter how much he encouraged them to study the scriptures for themselves (eating healthily) they seemed more content to come to the meetings to pick up small morsels of truth, direction and understanding.

Certainly in the history of Christianity individual studying of the scriptures was frowned upon and discouraged by the religious leaders. It was not for the layperson to read the Holy Scriptures for themselves. It was necessary for the trained clergy to interpret for the congregation.

Prior to the 1380's the Bible was only available in Latin and could only be read and interpreted by the Laity.

It took over two centuries[1] starting in the 1380's with John Wycliffe, an Oxford professor, scholar, and theologian who first translated the Bible into English before it commonly became available.

In John's gospel chapter *21v21-23* we have a biblical equivalent of Chinese whispers.

Peter sees the disciple John and asks Jesus, "What will John be doing?" Jesus replied:

> *'If I want him to remain alive until I return, what is*
> *that to you? You must follow me.'*

As a result of this, a rumour went out and the end version of that statement became

> *'John would not die'*

If you and I are going to get a right understanding of truth, if we are to protect ourselves from falling into the trap of following traditional teaching we must go back to the original source. This original source is God Himself.

Jesus makes the bold statement in *Matthew 12v28*

> *'Come to me, all you who are weary and burdened, and*
> *I will give you rest. Take my yoke upon you and learn of*

> *me, for I am gentle and humble in heart and you will
> find rest for your soul.'*

He also lamented that people failed to come to Him directly in
John 5v39-40.

> *'You diligently search the scriptures because you think
> that they possess eternal life. These are the scriptures
> that testify about me, yet you refuse to come to me to
> have life.*

Interestingly the true source is not even the Bible, as this has passed
through many levels of translations and interpretations. The true
source is God Himself.

It would be very remiss of me to suggest that religious leaders
should not instruct their congregations about the truth of scripture.
But what I am saying is that leaders should take exceptional care to pass
on the truth as carefully as they can, to create as near as possible a true
interpretation to the original.

Nowhere better is this illustrated than in *James Chapter 3.* This
chapter should be read carefully by everyone in its entirety.

Like most scriptures, more than one lesson can be drawn from what
is written. One meaning that comes clearly to my mind is symbolically
described in the chapter.

The tongue is likened to the rudder of a boat. In comparison to the
boat it is a small but a very important key part. The chapter begins by
stating the responsibility of teachers to get their instructions correct.

Symbolically the tongue is the teacher. What it teaches has the
power to direct the whole congregation. It will set the course and
direction for every student in his/her class.

Here now we see how easy the birth of the terrorist can be. If the teaching is wrong it corrupts the whole body and sets the whole course of life on fire, and is itself set on fire by hell.

There are no punches pulled here by James. This is serious stuff. How else can men say that they are doing the will of God but yet can in the next breath justify acts of terrorism. *Verse 9-10.*

> *'With the tongue (by the teacher) we praise our Lord and Father, and with it we curse men... out of the same mouth comes praise and cursing.'*

A good teacher should always be seeking to direct his/her students to the original. Like John the Baptist, teachers should know that their role is to point people towards the true light. The light that lights everyman that comes into the world.

Dear reader my heart's desire and prayer is that everyone for themselves can state with conviction and assuredly

1.   I know what I believe

2.   I know why I believe it.

Thy Kingdom come on earth as it is in Heaven.

CHAPTER 6

THE KEY IS REALITY

The key to fighting this duel is 'Reality'. I have already mentioned in the introduction that **The Duel** can be considered a fight between Reality and Theory.

Have all the theory you like in the world about God, the purpose of life, etc, but without real personal experience it counts for nothing! <u>Talk</u> about having the love of God in your heart, make an endless list of sacrifices you may have made during your life, but without the reality of experiencing God's love, it all counts for nothing.

The great sticking point along our journey back to God, the great deception, is when we think our theory, our much studying, our intelligence, our understanding is the same as the experimental reality. The two are simply not the same. Yet countless, thousands, millions of people down throughout the ages failed to see this crucial difference. 1 Corinthians Chapter 13 is an excellent description pointing out the difference between these two things.

Even if what you mentally ascent to and understand is true, it does not make it *real for you* unless you experience it. I could give example after example to illustrate this. You could be starving or perhaps never have tasted a particular type of food. With good articulate skill aided with excellent pictures and diagrams, I could describe to you in mouth-watering detail a new recipe. I could tell you the ingredients required, the preparatory stages, how to mix it, cook it etc. My teaching could be so good that your taste buds are fired up with expectation. You may even pass an exam in doing the work yourself by memorising and putting down on paper all I have taught you. If however, you have never tasted it, you miss out on the most important step of all – experience, or the reality of tasting for yourself. For all you know, what I 'rave' about may prove of no interest to you, more over, you may totally dislike it.

You may be the brightest student of all time, able to absorb in detail with total memory recall, everything there is to know about the brain from books etc, however, if you have no practical experience at all you may be hard pressed to find a patient willing to commit themselves to you in an operation. Laugh as you may about these examples, but look below the surface of these analogies and you will find that for most people, most of their Christian walk is based on theory not reality.

Preachers and teachers of Christian doctrine encourage (and rightly so) would-be believers to *taste and see* for themselves. They speak with eloquence, warning that God has no grandchildren, only children i.e., personal experience of being *'born again'*. But after this, the encouragement to experience for yourself falls off the higher the believer seeks to climb.

As you journey back to God, do all the study and searching that you can, but do not fall into the trap of thinking that 'head knowledge' is the same as 'really knowing'. Everything remains as *maybe* until you prove it, experiment for yourself until it becomes your personal reality.

Let's put what I have been saying in this chapter to the test right now. If I ask you what you believe to be the truth about the Christian understanding of the Holy Trinity, what would you answer? In fact, before you read on, why not stop, get a sheet of paper and write down your answers to the following three questions:

1.   Describe the Holy Trinity
2.   Do you believe in the Holy Trinity
3.   Why do you believe in the Holy Trinity

Go ahead and do this right now, before proceeding on.

All I ask in this is the privacy and openness of your own heart. Answer the question honestly for yourself.

****

How the Trinity came to be embraced is probably unknown by most who recite it week by week in Christian Churches. It came about as follows:

[1]Tertullian, a lawyer and presbyter of the third century Church in Carthage, was the first to use the word 'Trinity' when he put forth the theory that the Son and the Spirit participate in the being of God, but all are of one being of substance with the Father.

During the reign of the Emperor Constantine, Christian divisions were occurring across his Empire, in particular what was understood by the word Trinity. In order to enhance his political support Constantine realised it was important to unite these groups.

To gain unity amongst the Christians, Constantine called a

meeting of leading Bishops throughout the Roman Empire. The meeting took place at Nicene in A.D. 325.

Here the doctrine of the Trinity and other points of Christian theology were hammered out. The final 'unifying' agreement became known as the Nicene Creed. This Creed is famous amongst Christian Churches all over the world and states:

"We believe in one God, the Father Almighty, maker of all things visible and invisible; and in one Lord Jesus Christ, the Son of God, the only begotten of His Father, of the substance of the Father, God of God, Light of Light, very God of very God, begotten, not made, being of one substance with the Father. By whom all things were made, both which be in Heaven and in Earth. Who for us men and for our salvation came down (from Heaven) and was incarnate and was made man. He suffered and the third day He rose again, and ascended into Heaven. And He shall come again to judge both the quick and the dead. And (we believe) in the Holy Ghost. And whosoever shall say that there was a time when the Son of God was not, or that before He was begotten He was not, or that He was made of things that were not, or that He is of a different substance or essence (from the Father) or that He is a creature, or subject to change or conversion all that so say, the Catholic and Apostolic Church anathematizes them."[2]

The debate took place over six-weeks during which time there were many heated exchanges. At one stage Airus, one of the bishops, was punched in the face by Nicholas of Myra.[3] Arius was very much against the Creed in its final format and hence today 'Arianism' has become a catch phrase for anyone opposed to it.

In A.D. 451 at the council of Chalcedon the Creed was finally approved by the Pope and became an authorative statement. To disagree with the Creed was now considered blasphemy carrying a sentence ranging from mutilation to death.

Most of the Christian Churches today believe in the Holy Trinity on the basis of this historical fact. In short, repetition down through history has given this understanding a cornerstone in the Christian basis of faith! Repetition of anything does not make it a reality but it does confirm the theory and *'proves it beyond doubt...'* It took thousands of years to shift the popular historical thinking that the earth was flat! Amazing but true. A wrong understanding, however popular, however long it has been propagated does not make it right.

Just recently, a most renowned consultant in paediatrics in the United Kingdom (and perhaps the World) was struck off the medical register for severe professional misconduct. His evidence wrongly convicted and sent to prison, several women for allegedly killing their babies. In summing up, the General Medical Council made the statement that:

> *'The serious and fundamental nature of his errors were further <u>compounded</u> by his <u>repeated</u> use of the erroneous statistics'.*

I have not mentioned this case to embarrass the doctor or his family. It is really the General Medical Council's statement that is of interest here. While understanding and feeling the pain of those wrongly convicted, I also recognise and respect the colleagues of the doctor in question, who stood by him and pointed out his excellent history of work with babies, that saved many lives.

Many people today believe erroneous *'truth'* because it has been repeated relentlessly down through the ages of time. To escape this deception, each and every one should hold all they are taught as theory, until they can prove it for themselves.

There is no need to react one way or the other. Simply come to God with a heart that wants to know the truth,

> *"Ask, and it will be given unto you; seek, and you will find; knock, and the door will be opened unto you."*
> *Matthew 7v7*

No doubt will remain, no external ratification will be required,

> *"you will know the truth and the truth will set you free."*
> *John 8v32*

You may, in human terms, be considered inadequate, you may have been called an under-achiever, but concerning spiritual truth, all can graduate with first class honours.

> *"When they saw the courage of Peter and John and realised that they were unschooled, ordinary men, they were astonished and they took note that these men had been with Jesus." Acts 4v13*

NB. In using the Trinity question as an example, I am not stating that to believe in the Trinity is wrong. If you look back to the section 'A Message to You', I clearly state that this is not about changing your views on theology, the point is to challenge you to 'think it through for yourself'.

I leave this chapter with one final thought. Today I walked around a well-known Christian bookshop at a well-known seaside resort. Like on many of these occasions, I saw thousands of books on thousands of topics to do with the Christian faith. I could not help but wonder how many speak from the point of theory and how many speak from the point of reality.

If they speak from the point of theory only, are they compounding error by repetition? Settle for nothing in your life less than reality.

> *'He came as a witness to testify concerning that light, so that through him all men might believe'* 1 John 5v13

Chapter 7

What is that to you? Follow me

Every good parent recognises that the children they have are not theirs, as things to own or possess. Good parents should be on the lookout to recognise their child's unique abilities and talents, then to encourage them in that direction.

Successful parenting will result in the child severing links in due time with the parents, to go on and fulfil that unique life. If a parent tries to force the child into a mould of their choosing, the child may well live an unfulfilled and often emotionally distressed life. Equally, if a parent fails to let a child grow up and move away in the process of time, the child is again not able to function properly in life. We call such a child *'tied by the apron strings'*.

I have read about offspring 'trapped' in careers of their parents choosing, who come to understand their right to individuality. Helped by this knowledge, they have found the strength and determination to break free and follow their dream, their true destiny.

In the main, the Church today in the 21st Century, still needs to learn the lesson of *'letting its children go'*. The Church loves every newborn newcomer, they love to help in the shaping and development, but almost refuse to let the children go – not a new problem. Moses had the same problem way back in the Old Testament. *Exodus 5v1.*

The moment the growing Christian wants to step out on its own and choose a path not to the Church's liking or thinking, every effort is made to inhibit and stifle this emerging soul. No wonder the Church lacks both power and authority in today's world. Church members are on the decline and Churches are scratching around to find some sort of gimmicky way to attract new members. Yet, we live in a time when spiritual hunger has not declined amongst people. Many see the Church as irrelevant and out of touch and are turning to other means to fulfil the spiritual void they have. Before you think I exaggerate the situation, this is the same problem that Jesus charged the Church of His day with.

> *"They tie up heavy loads and put them on men's shoulders, but they themselves are not willing to lift a finger to move them." Matthew 23v4*

Every single life is totally unique. General principles can and need to be taught by the Church, but there must come a time when that uniqueness can only be taught and directed by God Himself. The disciples worked with Jesus for three years. In that time, their education was mainly general, the principle applied to all of them. Towards the end of Jesus' mission on earth He gives to Peter a very specific and personal message – *John 21v15-19.* Peter looking around and seeing John asks *"Lord, what about him?" John 21v21* Jesus gives an amazing answer. In today's modern idiom he simply says …..

> *'Mind your own business, what I have to say to John has nothing at this point to do with you… you only need*

concern yourself about what I have to say and ask of you'
John 21v22

The Apostle Paul gives us another good example of this in *Acts 15*. The Jews had the Laws of Moses. Amongst these laws was the law of circumcision. The need for circumcision was a fundamental command and a founding cornerstone that symbolically showed the Jews' commitment to God. Not to be circumcised would mean a rejection of the God of Abraham Isaac and Jacob. This was a major, major doctrine of the day.

The Apostle Paul is called by God to take the Gospel of salvation to the Gentiles. In his personal call, Paul is not required to teach or insist on circumcision. When the Jewish Christians hear of this there is total uproar. A fierce argument develops; they are literally arguing over the souls of men! A big meeting of all the founding leaders of the Christian Church is called and a great debate ensues. Fortunately, there are some Jewish believers, who understand the mind of God. As their words filled with power and authority are heard, the confirmation of Paul's unique calling is understood and prevails. The account of the whole incident is worth reading and its implications worth considering carefully. *Acts 15v1-29.*

On another occasion the apostle Peter assumes a spokesperson role on behalf of the Church. He is taking his personal call from Jesus to look after the emerging Church seriously. God has a special mission for Peter to speak to Cornelius, a man searching after the truth. There is only one problem, Cornelius was a Roman citizen. As far as the Jews were concerned the Romans were outside the chosen nation and an occupying force. For Peter to take the message of Christ to Cornelius would be considered as heresy. To get Peter to do this important job, a symbolic vision is given to him. After much hesitation and uncertainty

Peter does as he is requested and Cornelius and many other Romans enter into a personal understanding of God. You can read the full account in *Acts 10 and 11*.

On both these occasions it was absolutely important and necessary for the Jews to think outside of the box. They had to put aside dogma, tradition and history. It cannot be underestimated how much of a duel took place on both these occasions. Every time I think of a modern equivalent of what was involved I hesitate, feeling the ripple effects of the duel.

Perhaps the Church of England needs to weigh its debate about women ordination and homosexual relationships in light of this. If God is in these things, then it will prevail, lest ironically we be found fighting against God Himself. Individuals must face the challenge of ***The Duel*** and decide, whether they will serve men or God ... *Acts 4v18-22.*

On the larger scale of things leaders and/or members of different cultural faiths are going to have to take steps like those illustrated above if the human race is to move forward and journey back to God.

I love the Scriptures. If we have eyes to see and ears to hear and open hearts, we will not go far wrong. The traditional Church must learn the lesson, not to force its thinking on to others. It must remain open to hear what God is currently doing in our time. We must all learn to hear from God ourselves.

> ***"See I am doing a new thing, do you not perceive it?"*** *Isaiah 43:19*

CHAPTER 8

THE EMPEROR'S CLOTHES AND THREE MEN ON AN ISLAND - HOW TO AVOID DECEPTION

I would think that most, if not everyone reading this book has heard of the tale of the Emperor and his new clothes written by Hans Christian Andersen in 1837.

Very briefly the tale is of an Emperor conned by two men who claimed to be master weavers who could make clothes for the Emperor, of great quality and design. The clothes would be made of very special material that could only be seen by people who were wise and of the highest integrity. Anyone stupid or not fit for their post would not be able to see the clothes.

The Emperor was duped because of his vanity and all the others were duped either because they were stupid or did not want to appear as stupid. It took a young boy who was innocent enough to see what he saw and tell it like it was, that brought everyone else to their senses.

When you read or hear this tale you cannot help but smile that anyone could be so gullible as the Emperor, his trusted friends and the general public at large.

No one ever likes to admit that they have been duped. So much so that many who are victims of such fraud do not even report the matter to the police or authorities. This reluctance is due to fear. The fear of being further ridiculed for being so 'obviously foolish.' They do not come forward to avoid, as they see it, adding insult to personal injury.

It is sad to say, that many people today run the risk of falling victim to the same kind of deception when it comes to matters of religious belief. Somewhere in the back of such individual's minds is a niggle, an uncertainty, as to where they align with a point of view or doctrine. This hesitancy, this doubt is brushed aside however, because the majority of people around them appear to go along with it. They therefore keep quiet and suppress such concerns to avoid appearing ignorant and foolish.

I was reminded recently of Galileo's discovery in his day that the earth was not the centre of the universe, and that the sun and other planets did not orbit around the earth. This discovery was contrary to the popular religious opinion of his day. The Church judged Galileo's findings as heresy and contrary to the teachings of Holy Scripture. He was forced to retract his findings or face death. That is quite an incentive to comply with group thinking. [1]

Although people who stand up for what they feel and think may not be put under the threat of death (some sadly still are) the fear and pressure to comply can certainly feel as great.

Ironically the greater the religious zeal of a person the greater is their vulnerability to this type of deception.

The Apostle Paul said in *Romans 10v1-3*

'Brethren, my heart's desire and prayer to God for Israel is that they may be saved. For I bear them witness that they have a zeal for God, but not according to knowledge. For they being ignorant of God's righteousness, and seeking to establish their own righteousness, have not submitted to the righteousness of God.'

Have you ever been in a situation where you were afraid to say what you really thought because everyone else appeared to think differently? When you find yourself in a similar situation it always comes as a great relief to realise that you are not alone in your thinking or your viewpoint.

As a young lad growing up I remember hearing a sermon where the preacher said that believers should be like salmon, prepared to swim against the tide of worldly standards and make a stance for biblical standards. To drive the point home the preacher added that any dead fish could go with the tide but only a live fish could swim against the current. These words are certainly worth taking note of and applying in our lives but are we guilty of failing in this very area when it comes to being honest with ourselves?

While writing this chapter of the book a new 10-day reality TV programme had just been screened in the UK. The programme called *"Space Cadets"* attracted a large audience during it's screening on Channel 4.[2]

The reality programme started top secret filming in March 2005 to find 9 volunteers to train and send into space. The trip into space would take place in December and the hoax would be filmed live. None of the candidates were aware that this was to be a real life "Truman show"[3]

As part of the illusion the cadets were told that the shuttle would take off horizontally. Food and some of the props were bought and specially flown in from Russia. A Russian fitness trainer would take them through a vigorous training programme.

The spaceship was constructed from the set used in the film Space Cowboys[4] starring Clint Eastwood, made originally from a NASA blueprint.

The cockpit had four windows, which in reality were giant digital screens, which used graphics three times the resolution of high definition TV. The effects produced were better than that created in the film The Matrix[5].

A Lecturer in Astronautics at Kingston's University by the name of Chris Welch was responsible for educating the Cadets about space. Most of the facts fed to the students were true but about 20% of what they were told for the purpose of the show was false. Chris Walsh commented that

> *'Interestingly, the cadets rarely question any of the false information, but find it hard to believe many of the genuine facts!'*

During the final episode the Cadets are told the truth about the hoax. Naturally they are embarrassed by the fact that they have been 'had' but all of them reported moments when they knew something was not quite right and/or had their suspicions!

So even here it is shown that it is very hard to break free of a deception that everyone around you seems involved in.

In **'The Duel'** I am not suggesting that religion is trying to dupe anyone into believing a lie. In reality I am suggesting that most of the world is caught up in a delusion that has no author but ourselves, time and tradition. In a sense our deception is worse because we are self-propagating the delusion and are not aware that this is the case!

The Apostle warns that we must wake up in *Ephesians 5v14.*

Jesus says a similar thing in *John 9v4.*

> *'If you were blind, you would not be guilty of sin; but now that you claim you can see, your guilt remains.'*

Time and time again Jesus urges those that have eyes to use them to see the truth and those that have ears to use them to listen for the truth.

THE THREE MEN ON AN ISLAND

One means we have for waking up is by looking very closely and observing how people around us are acting. From time to time the *'Space Cadets'* were aware that some of the people around them (the actors in on the hoax) made slight slip ups.

As a lad I also heard a paradox of three men shipwrecked on a small island. These three men believed they were the only survivors. While they were asleep under a tree one day, sheltering from the powerful rays of the noonday sun, a young rascal hiding up the tree shinned down and painted the face of each man black. When the men awoke they all started laughing. Suddenly after a few minutes of merriment one of the men stopped laughing.

In the book relating this parable the question is asked 'why did one man stop laughing so abruptly'? Well I will leave you to do the logic bit, but short to say the one who stopped laughing realised his face must be black as well.

With regard to this paradox, it is possible to realise that we may be part of a deception or misapprehension, if we observe our behaviour in relation to the behaviour of others around us.

If only we could allow our circumstances to become a mirror for ourselves. What a difference it could make.

Every now and then it would do us good to question our attitude and stance on any issue we act passionately about. Our actions should bear a direct relationship to our proven point of conviction. At the same time our actions should be tempered by any doubts we have, no matter how deep the doubt is rooted.

Jesus made a startling yet obvious statement as recorded in *Matthew 15v14* about the blind leading the blind.

> *'Leave them; they are blind guides. If a blind man leads a blind man, both will fall into a pit.'*

Do you have the courage to break free; can you see what is happening around you?

The struggle to break free is all bound up in *'The Duel'*

CHAPTER 9

THE PART THAT THE SCRIPTURES PLAY

If we are talking about breaking free of traditional expectations into the freedom of individual calling, as duelling, then the part that the scriptures play is beyond a doubt one of *'close combat'*. In the scriptures, the written word is referred to as *'the sword of the Spirit'*. It declares that it is sharper than any two edged sword. *Hebrews 4v12.*

In close combat, we need to know how to wield the sword expertly to break free of the chains that would shackle us to tradition and prison. A wrong move here could not only see us receive a fatal wound from those who seek to hold us prisoner, but if we are not careful, we can do damage to ourselves in the process.

Scriptures tell us many things about the written word, but we will look at four things in particular:

1.   It is not for personal interpretation
2.   It needs to be rightfully interpreted
3.   It is able to separate soul from spirit
4.   Make us wise unto salvation

Lets look at these aspects

1. It is not for personal interpretation 2 Peter 1v20

The fact that we have so many interpretations of key parts of the Bible shows that in terms of the bigger picture we have not done very well in this area. In close combat, we have succeeded in dividing up the Body of Christ into many warring parts.

As a young Christian growing up, this anomaly always had a strong impact on my thinking. Different schools of thought all argued their case, very eloquently, quoting numerous Scriptures to confirm their point of belief. Each side could boast very eminent and recognised leaders, who certainly had great skills in presentation and oratory.

The stage in my mind was set out like a Court of Law. Defence and Prosecution took up the case with vigour at a libel hearing. Scriptures were called to the bar as witnesses to give evidence. The cases have now gone on for centuries, moving up the hierarchy of the legal system from court to court, from appeal to appeal right up to the House of Lords. Many books have been written to support the claims of each side.

Like all libel cases, they are very costly and neither side wins! The Church is drained of its authority, and sidelined in its main aim. As I mentioned earlier, the Church of England is currently engaged in two such 'libel actions':

    (a)   Women ordination

    (b)   Gay rights

As these cases rumble on, two things are certain:

    1. It will tear the Church apart

    2. Those looking on will find another way

What then is the answer to this tricky problem? Unravelling the Scriptures is not a task for the *intellectual mind* but the *enlightened* mind. Truth is not something you can 'force' into someone by logic or academic means, but truth is something that the Spirit of God reveals to each person from within. *John 14v26.*

Therefore 'unlearned men' like James and John could confound the religious establishment of their day. The Scriptures cannot be understood by intellect, which can only go around the outside of the truth.

If the Church focuses on making disciples, each one will be persuaded of the 'truth' as he or she grows in stature with God. This is how wisdom of the Scriptures is gained ...

"Jesus grew in wisdom and stature ......" Luke 2v52

2. Scriptures need to be rightfully interpreted 2 Timothy 2v15

Make a statement about your understanding of Scripture to a group of people that hold a different viewpoint and you may well find you are accused of not 'rightfully interpreting' Scripture. This is the sort of statement aimed at bringing you back into line with group thinking.

As a young believer growing up, I came to the conclusion that the Scriptures could be used to justify almost anything! Even murder! A quick look at history will confirm this. In fact, why look back into history, you have only to look at current events happening around the world today:

Northern Ireland

Israel/Palestine

The War on Terrorism

Examine each of these carefully and one common thread runs through each:

All believe they are defending a *'God given'* directive to rid the world of an error or put more bluntly, they are defending an interpretation of Holy Scripture (each group has their Holy Scriptures). No wonder the World looking on says it wants nothing to do with religion (and politics – as most religions give rise to its politics!)

From the Christian viewpoint, Christ is the example we can unite around. I often found myself smiling whilst reading the Gospels. On many occasions, the Scribes and Pharisees would quote the Scripture at Jesus to point out His errors. Interestingly, Jesus never refuted what they quoted, but answered always by quoting another Scripture!

Do you see the 'close combat' situation? This comes to a head when Jesus points out to the Scribes and Pharisees, that they were in error because they did not understand the Scriptures! *Matthew 22v29*

Here is a big big big clue, not to be missed.

> *'… study the Scriptures, because you think that by them you possess eternal life… yet you refuse to come to me to have life!' John 5v39.*

Scripture is not for personal interpretation and must be rightfully interpreted. To do this you must first learn of Christ.

> *'Take my yoke upon you and learn of me.' Matthew 11v29.*

Each person must personally come to Christ to learn

> *'..When they saw the courage of Peter and John and realised that they were unschooled, ordinary men, they were astonished and they took note that these men had been with Jesus..' Acts 4v13*

Let me give you an acid test to help you know if you have 'the truth'.

Truth (love) does not demand its own way.

Truth (love) never overrides someone else's free will.

See any group that forces – however covertly – its point of view onto others and even if the point is true it comes from a corrupt source and should be avoided.

> *In modern day parlance Jesus said, "The teachers of the law and the Pharisees sit in Moses' seat. So you must obey them and do everything they tell you. But do not do what they do, for they do not practise what they preach." Matthew 23v2-3*

To the leaders of the West, I give this warning. You cannot bomb a people into submission. To the leaders of the Eastern cultures, do not force an interpretation of your Holy Scriptures on to young vulnerable minds. These are not the ways of God, they are not the way of love, they are not the way of peace, they are not the way of hope.

3. Scriptures separate soul from spirit Hebrews 4v12

This could also be written as separating the Ego from The Self. In very basic terms, the Ego is all about self-interest with a small 's'. It is all about 'me', 'mine' and 'I'. Generally speaking, Ego is about selfishness. Self with a capital 'S' is about the 'real' you. Self is that part of us which is truly spiritual and eternal. It is that part of us which is the true likeness of God. It is the 'bruiser of the serpent' *Genesis 3v15*. It is the true light which lights every man that comes into the world *John 1v9*

The best, most succinct definition of the Ego and Self I have read is by Deepak Chopra in his book the 'Seven Spiritual Laws of Success'[1]. In biblical terms the fall is when the Ego usurped authority over the Self. Redemption is about restoring the true Self to its rightful position above the Ego.

In this close combat, the sword (The Word) has the ability to reach down past the Ego to where the Self lies buried, piercing and allowing the light of God to reach through. The sword is able to cut away endless layers and trappings, not least the trappings of tradition and dogma. As the spirit is reached and uncovered, so wisdom, love, faith and every good attribute is awakened within us.

From a human nature perspective interpreting the will of another is extremely difficult. I have witnessed situations (you may have personal similar examples you have experienced) where interpreting the 'Will' of a close dead relative can be traumatic to say the least. Families have been divided over such matters refusing to even talk for years to their own 'flesh and blood'. Each party was sure that their interpretation was the correct one.

When it comes to interpreting God's Word, different groups end up in the same disastrous situation, falling out and accusing the other of wrong interpretation.

The same problem is endemic throughout society. Lord Donaldson (Master of the Rolls from 1982 to 1992 and now sits as a Crossbench peer in the House of Lords) made the following statement concerning interpreting the will of Parliament.[2]

> *"the Judiciary's job is to interpret the will of Parliament. All Governments confuse their will with the will of Parliament. This Government is no exception.*
>
> *The job of Judge's is to ensure that the Government of the day does not exceed its powers, which is a permanent desire, unconscious no doubt, of all Governments."*

There is only one thing worse than trying to interpret the Scripture for someone else, that is to force our interpretation onto him or her.

4. "... The holy Scriptures which are able to make you wise for salvation...." 2 Timothy 3v14-17

As a final thought to this chapter let me leave you with this idea that came to me during the final editing stages of this book.

If you interpret the scriptures wrong you are in error. If you interpret it correctly there are many who will tell you that you are still wrong. Jesus said as much himself: *'...in fact a time is coming when anyone who kills you will think he is offering a service to God...' John 16v2*

Come on thinking people, how do we solve this paradox? Instead of forcing our interpretation onto others we need to allow each person the freedom to think for themselves. We must trust that God who instructs us can instruct and direct another equally well. For now we need to focus on what is important. In the chapter 'The Chicken and the Egg Syndrome' this idea is further developed.

And what does the Lord require of you? To act justly and to love mercy and to walk humbly with your God. Micah 6v8.

CHAPTER 10

THE OLD TESTAMENT VS THE

NEW TESTAMENT

I recently read an interesting story in a book called 'Discover the Power Within You' by Eric Butterworth.[1]

A young boy attending Sunday School had many lessons and stories from the Old Testament. After many weeks, the class started looking at the New Testament. The lad came home and said to his parents, *"God sure got better as He got older ..."*

If you are a totally honest person and have read all the Old and New Testament objectively without bias, you may have ended up making the same statement as the young boy. You may be left with some feeling of discrepancy between the two sections. The God of the Old Testament seems like a capricious, vengeful, warlike God, while the God of the New appears like a God full of compassion, loving, merciful, etc.

If you take into account statements in the Bible like *"God is the same yesterday, today and forever"* your confusion may be compounded. So has God changed and got better with time? Jesus said He had not come to change the law but to fulfil it.

It is very important that each individual believer reconcile their understanding of the Old and New Testament clearly for themselves. Failure to do so could lead us to act, speak and think in ways inconsistent with spiritual maturity. This is one of the questions that we may have put on 'the back burner' and pushed out of our mind; one of those issues which niggles us from time to time.

One area of inconsistency is our response to other faith scriptures. For example here in the 21st Century, the western Christian Church may be keen to condemn the teaching of the Muslim faith that appears to encourage the use of the sword to ensure the spread of Islam. Its memory appears very short. It forgets that God through Joshua ordered the complete destruction of the 'heathen' nations who were at that time occupying the Promised Land. They were ordered to leave none alive, neither men, women nor children. (*Deuteronomy 2v33-34*). Imagine how that would read in today's papers. Sky news would have a field day and every political pressure would be brought to bear to encourage the Jewish people to root out such radical elements.

The truth is that there are still many in the western Christian Churches that would not hesitate to take up the sword to defend the Gospel and the faith as they see it. It may be helpful to say that in my view the Scriptures is a coherent book that holds together. If read with the mind of Christ, has the power to transform men and women into the very image of God. It is able to make us wise unto salvation.

If you want to pursue a Spiritual answer to the question of reconciling the Old and New Testament, then I suggest reading 'How to know God' by Deepak Chopra.[2]

May I just remind the reader that I am not trying to undermine the Christian faith or introduce new doctrine. I wish only that each person close the gap between theory and reality for themselves; to help free men and women from the slavery of tradition and hearsay. To allow each and every person direct access to God. that they may become what he wants them to be; to fulfil their true calling.

The reality is that God is not changing; He is love, goodness, and kindness. These are His attributes. He can never act from any other basis. Rather it is man who is evolving, making his journeying as a whole back to God.

We have reached the point in man's evolution where we must move past the prejudice of traditional thinking, fundamentalism and dogma. We must break through the bonds that have held us prisoner for generations. The time has come for the prison doors that hold the Church back to be opened, God is calling to the leaders:

"let my people go ..."Exodus 5v1.

If I am right, we will discover that this message is being repeated in every culture and every nation. The message is being brought to all people everywhere. If the traditional Church does not respond, it will find itself bypassed. The words of Christ will ring out again.

'But many who are first will be last, and the last first.'
Mark 10v31

CHAPTER 11

THE PART LEGISLATION AND

LAW PLAYS

In an earlier part of this book I stated that each person is a unique individual, with a unique gifting and must be free to follow their heart wherever it leads them; free of any kind of peer pressure to conform to another person or group's wishes. I have also reminded the reader of the famous saying, 'no man is an island.'

These are not contradictory statements but rather two halves that make up a great truth and principle that lead to the harmonious living together of people.

A mature spiritual person holds these two tensions in perfect balance.

The Apostle Paul summarises this balanced maturity in Romans chapter 14 and 15. In particular he says,

> *'Let us therefore make every effort to do what leads to peace and to mutual edification' Romans 14v19*

> 'Each of us should please his neighbour for his good, to build him up' Romans 15v2

Legislation and law (in the remainder of this chapter I will refer to these two under the heading of just law) are one of the means that help us as human beings to balance the two statements mentioned above, and as a result help society move forward in a cohesive manner.

The fact that we need law is a sign of society's need to grow spiritually. Think about it for a moment. If everyone lived their own lives with a genuine consideration for their neighbour there would be no need for laws. No one would think of taking that which does not belong to him or her. No one would seek to injure another. We would drive on the roads with courtesy and consideration for other roads users. The list could just go on and on.

Although this may seem idealistic this is the goal that mankind wants to reach, it is the goal that God is moving the world towards.

Old Testament law, summarised as the Ten Commandments, were only given to man as a schoolmaster or caretaker for a limited period of time.

The law is required only until the world comes to spiritual maturity.

> 'So the law was put in charge to lead us to Christ that we might be justified by faith. Now that faith has come, we are no longer under the supervision of law.' Galatians 3v24-25

All law 'terminates' and is no longer required when we love God and love our neighbour as ourselves. Spiritual maturity is like the dawning of the new day. Darkness (law) is hidden and becomes invisible when the sun (love) rises in the sky. The law remains but is not perceived. *Matthew 22v35-40*

At the time of writing, the world has not reached this type of spiritual maturity. This is evident; therefore the law has a vital part to play. However, I do have a great concern about how the law is perceived, interpreted and meted out.

1. The law is a blunt instrument

Firstly as the law is a temporary measure, we must understand that in itself it is not perfect and has great limitation. At best it is a blunt instrument. Like any blunt instrument it can be used with only limited effectiveness. It is a useful tool for the broad picture, but is a poor choice when it comes to the details.

In Charles Dickens' novel 'Oliver Twist' the statement is made that 'The law is an Ass.' This is another way of saying that the law is a blunt instrument.

If justice and proper judgment is to be carried out, then law must be used in conjunction with its equal partner 'common sense.'

If we attempt to carry out the law strictly to the letter, then there will be many cases of miscarriage of justice. We see this all too often when cases are thrown out and crime goes unpunished because of a technical issue, or some innocent person is convicted when clearly common sense shows this is absurd. When it comes to the details, what is needed is not the letter of the law, but rather the 'spirit' of the law.

Jesus was a great champion for promoting the understanding that the spirit of the law was far more important than the letter of the law. Below are several examples where Jesus demonstrated this principle:

The woman caught in adultery John 8v3-11

According to the law the only act of justice was death by stoning for anyone committing adultery. When a woman was caught red handed in this crime the religious leaders brought her to Jesus to ask His view on what should be done. Really their actions were hypocritical and full of self-righteousness. Their motives were really to catch Jesus out. Jesus responded by kneeling down and writing in the sand (what He wrote is unknown) then simply asked that the person without sin should cast the first stone. One by one the righteous Scribes and Pharisees left until none of the accusers were left. Jesus' judgement to the woman was simple, 'go and sin no more'

The sheep falling into the pit on the Sabbath Matthew 12v9-13

According to the law no man should do any work of any kind on the Sabbath. This would be an act of disrespect towards God. On one Sabbath Jesus is in the Synagogue. Present, was a man with a withered hand. The religious leaders asked if it would be right to heal him (do work) on the Sabbath. Jesus responded by asking which of them who had a sheep that had fallen down in a pit would not stop and get it out immediately. To wait another day may have meant its death.

It is interesting that in all these cases it was the religious leaders who did not like the message of freedom and liberty. They were using the law to try and catch Jesus out. Are there any parallels we could learn from here?

2. The Nanny State phenomenon

I find it very interesting that God felt the need to only give ten laws for a whole nation to live by. These ten basic laws embody all that is required for any nation to live together in harmony and peace.

It is true that these ten laws, when interpreted, filled the book of Leviticus and Deuteronomy to 60 chapters of explanation and detail. However, the important principle of scripture is that <u>many</u> laws were not needed.

Jesus went on to condense the ten laws to just two! Love God and love your neighbour as yourself. *Mathew 22:37-40*

At the time of writing a relatively new phrase is becoming common currency in the UK, namely, that we are in danger of becoming a nanny state. By this phrase it is meant that governments seem to feel the need to create and interpret laws at an alarming rate, to deal with the issues of the day; I believe this danger is very real. How ironic that a free democratic nation is running headlong down the road to becoming a police state.

It may be argued that today's modern society needs more and more complex laws to maintain social cohesion. I disagree on the basis of two main reasons:

1. There is nothing new under the sun. Human nature does not change from one generation to another. Situations may be different, but at the heart of what we do is still the old human nature.

2. I subscribe to the principle that in thinking we are becoming wiser, we are in reality become more foolish. *Romans 1v22*. We have jokes circulating about political correctness gone mad. One that springs readily to mind is that we are in danger of renaming 'man-hole cover' to 'people-hole cover' so as not to offend.

When issues of the day arise and need to be dealt with, the government reaches into its 'bag of tools' and more often than not pulls out law as its first choice.

Here are some interesting statistics about the proliferation of laws being passed in the UK.

More than 32,000 statutory instruments have been passed since 1997.

Since 1997 Parliament has passed 23 criminal justice acts, five immigration acts, seven anti-terror laws, 10 education acts and 11 involving health and social care. The new laws, the Liberal Democrats claim, have created 3,000 criminal offences - almost one a day - and add up to 114,000 pages. That means Parliament has passed more than one page of legislation for every hour that Labour has been in office. [1]

3. Bad Laws increase tensions

More often than not most laws may not be popular with the people, but a far more important distinction needs to be made between a good law and a bad law.

Laws are rarely, if ever, neutral. They either help the cohesion of society or increase the tension.

Bad laws tend to be those that are arrived at hastily, usually as a knee jerk response to a situation. Sometimes they are no more than someone's personal preferences or a group preference by the back door.

This is one of the reasons why it is imperative that governments and the judiciary are totally independent. Those that make the law (the government) should not interfere with those who seek to interpret and carry out the law (the judiciary).

In the context of this book, laws are being passed that stifle people's individual right to be as they choose. To legislate how someone views someone else's religion or life style is almost certainly going to be a bad law. No legislation can force a viewpoint to be acceptable.

Everyone is fully entitled to have any combination of religious, ethical, moral or racial views, which they should be allowed to freely express. The problem only comes when an individual or group believes it can force that point of view to prevail. However, any law that seeks to prevent an individual or group from expressing their viewpoint, in my opinion, is a bad law.

A bad law will serve only to increase tension between individuals and groups.

What we normally refer to as prejudice is often only someone's point of view. Most attempts to legislate against prejudice is therefore, more likely than not, to stifle someone's free will of thought.

I am not afraid to say that I believe in God. Equally I am not afraid for someone else to come along and claim to be an atheist, or to blaspheme the name of God. I may be sad but not outraged.

I am not afraid if someone calls me names because my skin is brown, or suggests that I should 'go back to my own country of origin.' Again I may be saddened but not outraged.

Viewpoints are totally acceptable. Violence to achieve a point of view is totally unacceptable. The law has always had the power to deal with violence whatever its source.

> *'Let no debt remain outstanding, except the continuing debt to love one another, for he who loves his fellow-man has fulfilled the law. The commandments, "do not commit adultery," "Do not steal," "Do not covet," "and whatever other commandment there may be, are summed up in this one rule:" Love your neighbour as yourself." Love does no harm to its neighbour. Therefore love is the fulfilment of the law.' Romans 13v8-10*

CHAPTER 12

NEW WINESKINS

Most, if not all people have heard the saying *"hindsight is a wonderful thing…"* It is also a very true saying as well. It is always easy after the event to see if we made the right or wrong choices. Another saying that should be weighed carefully along with this saying is the one which says *"history teaches us nothing!"* We have all the benefit of history and hindsight yet it appears very difficult for us to see similarities in current parallel situations.

A classic example is given to us in the Scriptures in *Matthew 23v29-36.* In the Old Testament, God has sent many Prophets to Israel as a people and nation to repent and turn back to Him. However, these Prophets were not believed and some even killed by the people. By the time of Christ these Prophets were recognised as true 'Servants of God'. To correct the mistakes the Scribes and Pharisees had built special tombs to pay tribute to them. Standing in front of them is God's greatest Prophet, Jesus, who they are shortly to kill. They simply could not make use of hindsight or history to stop making the same mistake in their time.

How many more wars must we fight before we realise that the aftermath and tragedy of death accomplishes nothing? How many more acts of terrorism before we realise the bomb accomplishes nothing?

A new approach, a Spiritual approach is required. Jesus declared in His famous statement:

> *'And no-one pours new wine into old wineskins. If he does, the new wine will burst the skins, the wine will run out and the wineskins will be ruined.' Luke 5v37.*

Note, both the new wine and old wineskins are lost! Not only what is new does not profit, but the benefit of history is also lost.

Jesus' teaching required a new approach, a new response to His words. What God is doing today, all over the world, requires new wineskins. Calling for the new wineskin is always the point where rejection is likely to occur:

> *"And no-one after drinking old wine wants the new, for he says, 'The old is better.'" Luke 5v39*

Jesus was initially accepted, until He began to state what the new wine was; at this point the crowds turn against Him and many are offended. *John 6v66.*

Colloquially speaking, He had gone too far, He goes from wise Prophet to possessed Demonic supplanter. The same happened to the Apostle Paul. Everything is fine until he begins to speak his personal message of conviction.

> *"Your great learning is driving you insane." Acts 26v24*

This is a new wineskin moment – what choice will this generation make?

There are people today (and in every age) who have never heard the names we know God by or the message of the Gospel as we know it, but they do have a dynamic, real relationship with God.

> *"I have other sheep that are not of this pen:.."* John 10v16

This is new wine!

The true Self is very much alive in them and awake, they hear, know and obey the Voice of God – do you know how these pieces fit together? Yet for all this, I can still say without contradiction that Christ is the way back to God.

There are millions of people, from all ages and walks of life that from a traditional definition of a Christian, fall outside of the category. Yet they are truly in every sense and meaning of the word, enlightened and one with God.

On one occasion when Jesus is speaking to the crowds following Him, and warns that in Heaven He will be turning away many who thought they were working for Him even though they have done many apparent wonderful things in His name, He will declare he never knew them! *Matthew 7v21-23*

If you have ears to hear and eyes to see, hear and see what the Spirit of God is saying and sharing today.

> *"Behold! I am doing a new thing, do you not perceive it?"*

New wineskin or much learning has made me mad? You must decide for yourself. Listen to your heart, follow its prompting, it is the Self within you leading you to God.

Chapter 13

Are the Scriptures all that God has to Say?

As God is an infinite Being, without beginning and end, it goes without saying that absolutely no book, however 'Holy' it may be considered, can possibly be all that God has to say. In the Gospel of John, the writer is carried away by the excellency and Glory of God and pauses to make this most dramatic statement:

> '...I suppose that even the whole world would not have room for the books that would be written.' John 21v25

As every Being is truly a unique expression of God, it stands to reason that some things God has to say are directed personally to each individual. The Apostle Paul makes an amazing declaration in Acts:

> "He heard inexpressible things, things that man is not permitted to tell" 2 Corinthians 12 v 4

This simply means that not only are some things said to every individual directly by God, but some of those things may also be totally private, not for general repeating.

On at least one occasion, Jesus asked His Disciples not to tell anyone until an appointed time later, some of the things He had shared with them. *Matthew 17v1-9.*

In the Book of Revelations God has something specific and different to say to each of the seven Churches. *Revelations Chapters 2-3.* I have in an earlier chapter pointed out the possibility of deception, naturally that applies here also. Many atrocities that have occurred have been done 'in the name of God'. Many acts of wickedness have been done because people believed they were directly obeying the Voice of God. How can we safeguard ourselves and be confident that God has spoken to us?

I do not believe that the answer to this question is difficult, or complex. In fact, direct access to hearing God speak is available to every human being on the planet. In reality, our ability to hear God speak should be as natural and as second nature to us as breathing, eating or sleeping.

> *'For in him we live and move and have our being'. Acts 17v28.*

His Spirit dwells within us and bears witness with our Spirit. Not to hear the Voice of God is like a fish swimming in the ocean looking for the water!

As I mentioned earlier, the Self (the Spirit) is buried deep under the Ego (Soul) of man. The Word of God has the power to separate out the Spirit so that it can breathe and communicate again with God. So it is that the Word can make us wise unto salvation. We can be confident we are hearing God speaking as our character becomes more like God.

God is infinite wisdom, infinite patience, infinite love (1 Corinthians Chapter 13) as our lives align with these characteristics so the more clearly we will hear Him speak.

If any man hath ears to hear, let him hear what God is saying. The danger in the tradition of the established Christian Church is that it is considered the average man is not capable of hearing God for himself or that it hears on behalf of men and its duty is to pass on His instructions. Up to a point, this is fine. Paul talks about this general understanding in *Galatians 4v1*.

This is similar to a parent bringing up a child until it can (and must or might) take responsibility for itself. The Church should see itself only as a responsible parent or guardian. It was not that long ago when the ordinary man in the street was not allowed to read the Bible for himself, and still today, the established Church thinks that it has a right to dictate the policy of God to all its congregation. (Sure, it has a right to advise or suggest, but no authority to dictate).

Some branches of the Christian Church still believe it has authority to say what job a member may or may not do; who may marry who, how their money should be used. Such things only speak of fear and control instead of love and liberty. Western Government today stands at a new crossroads, where the state is in danger of becoming a dictator – ironically in the name of freedom and democracy.

We must find a better way. That way is faith and trust in a living God, who is able to do far more abundantly than we can ever ask or think. *Ephesians 3v20*.

"We need to let go and let God."

Around this issue hinges the birth of the fanatic, which in turn gives birth to the terrorist!

When an individual, or group of people or an organisation, or even a Government believes it must have its Will (viewpoint) enforced and obeyed, this becomes the fertile ground of fanaticism, from the fanatic it is a short step to the terrorist, who feels at whatever cost he must bring this viewpoint into reality – for the good of the cause. The only hope the world has of peace love and joy is in each man, woman and child learning to hear the words of the loving God directly for themselves.

His words bring life, His words bring love, His words bring hope, His words bring joy.

CHAPTER 14

DEALING WITH THE EVIDENCE AND DYSFUNCTIONALITY

How you deal with *'the evidence that comes your way'* is crucial to how you are fairing in *'The Duel'*.

It is important to understand how I am using the phrase *'the evidence that comes your way.'*

Throughout this book I have been suggesting that the closed mind fails to make progress in understanding truth. People with closed minds tend to seek out knowledge and evidence that only promote their particular point of view. At the same time they dismiss any evidence or facts that contradict their stance. They easily become agitated and often reject with ridicule or outrageous hostility, arguing any point of view not supporting their stance. They are simply not comfortable in hearing something they do not want to hear, or seeing something they do not want to see.

Whenever Jesus was opposed He was happy to explain His position but if rejected He was equally happy to simply move on. He saw no reason for heatedly or angrily defending His corner or His claims. Although He had a passion to persuade men and women to believe, He saw no reason to force His will or way of seeing things on others. This understanding He sought to pass onto His disciples.

> *'Whatever house you enter, stay there until you leave that town. If people do not welcome you, shake the dust off your feet when you leave their town, as a testimony against them.' Luke 9v4.*

I have found from experience that if we really want to know truth we only have to ask with an open heart and mind. God who is love and only wishes that everyone should come to know the truth, will work tirelessly to ensure we understand.

Jesus could not make this clearer when He says in *Matthew 7v7*.

> *'Ask and it will be given to you; seek and you will find; knock and the door will be opened to you. For everyone who asks receives; he who seeks finds; and to him who knocks, the door will be opened.'*

This loving God who wants us to understand truth will simply make the 'evidence come our way.'

It is important to realise that this knowledge is open to everyone. No-one is excluded. A degree is not needed; a formal education is not needed. How often we are told by those in 'high positions' of learning that we do not have the ability to understand. Jesus saw it differently. The disciples were attacked in court on the basis that they were unlearned men, too ignorant to know what they were talking about. *Acts 4v13*. Yet they prevailed when it was realised that they had been with Jesus.

One interesting thing that I have found is that 'asking' can take the form of any question. It does not have to be what we may think of as spiritual. God is interested in everything we do in life. If we have any question requiring a solution He will always answer if we ask.

The evidence that comes our way can take on an infinite number of forms and disguises. Sometimes the evidence hits us right between the eyes and is very hard to miss or argue against.

For example I remember once feeling unsettled about a job I was in. The job itself was fine and I enjoyed it immensely but something inside was telling me it was time to move on. The feeling was so strong that my wife and I took the day off to think through how I was feeling and what to do next. A week later I happened to mention to a friend, very casually, that I was interested in changing jobs. His eyes immediately lit up. He asked me if I was serious about this, to which I replied that I was. To my amazement he then told me of someone that we both knew who was interested in employing me and had only held back from asking because he felt sure I would turn down the offer. A casual, informal, meeting was set up by my friend and within about a month I was happy in the new job. I loved every moment of the job which I went on to do for the next six years.

Sometimes the evidence can be very subtle, crossing your path like a shadow and requires sensitivity to pick it up. This sort of answer can leave us initially with the feeling of uncertainty. Did I hear right or did I just imagine that? It does not matter, God will answer again until we are sure. With practice we will find that we hear these more subtle answers more easily. These more subtle answers always leave us with a deeper sense of certainty, fulfilment and most importantly peace. Jesus says in *John 10v27*

> '*My sheep listen to my voice; I know them, and they follow me.*'

Whichever way the answer comes when we pick up on it you are left with a deep-seated peacefulness and contentment. We are left with a knowing within ourselves that does not require debate, argument or outward confirmation.

This is the truth that Jesus talks about that sets us free.

> *'You shall know the truth and the truth shall set you free.' John 8v31.*

It is very common for our minds to put up quite a fight if the truth that is trying to reveal itself to us, contradicts something we have up until that point regarded as truth.

This is the nature of *'The Duel'.*

If we are honest with ourselves, examining the new evidence carefully with an open mind, challenging it at every turn if necessary, the new light will eventually take hold. At the same time we will either modify what we thought was right beforehand or reject it all together. More often than not an outright rejection of what we thought was true is not necessary, just a modification of that point of understanding. But these small changes often add up to a huge change in perspective.

Sherlock Holmes once said to Watson

> *'Once you eliminate all other possibilities, what's left, however improbable, must be the solution.'*

I am more comfortable with the following modified version of this quote:

> *'Once you eliminate all other possibilities, what's left, however improbable, <u>may</u> be the solution.'*

With the altering of one word, 'may' instead of 'must' be the solution, this is a good statement to bear in mind when seeking after truth. If we hold this in mind it helps us to see past our personal prejudices and blockages caused by traditional thinking.

Interesting how the change of a single word can make such a difference in our understanding.

Dysfunctionality

There is a certain type of dysfunctionality that can happen to people who hold strong religious convictions.

This section requires a short statement to help eliminate certain misunderstandings.

Please note that I use the words 'type' and 'can' therefore I am not in any way characterising all people with strong religious convictions into one mould.

Some people with religious convictions can at times find it difficult to know how to interact and behave in certain social situations. A simple example may help.

In the very first job I held back in the early 70's I was a salesman. As described in an earlier chapter, my upbringing was based on a strong Evangelical Pentecostal background. For me certain things were very clearly black or white.

The first meeting of all the area representatives in my sales department took place in a hotel and we broke for refreshments in the bar area. The fact that we were eating in the 'bar' area made me very uncomfortable. Somewhere in my subconscious being in a pub, or any place that sold alcohol was not the place to be. Places like this belong 'to the devil' and I was putting my soul in mortal danger. In that environment, at that time, I did not know how to function properly. I felt a strong need to point out to my colleges that this was wrong and we should go somewhere else. At very best I felt the need to introduce some form of witnessing which in hindsight may have helped to justify the situation.

On another occasion one of the ministers of a Church that I was once a member of, told me of an occasion at work where a young lady had just joined the company. This young lady was very keen to let everybody know that she had a faith in Jesus and they also needed to have the same faith. She believed this was the right thing to do and her approach would soon vindicate itself. Some months later she told my friend that things had not worked out and she would be leaving. Wisely, my friend took her to the side and explained that maybe it would be wiser to approach her next job in a calmer fashion and let her life do the talking rather than her words.

The type of dysfuntionality that I am thinking about that can affect religious people can show up in all areas of their lives. I personally notice it more where there is a social context. It can have disastrous effects in close relationships.

Those that have this type of problem at an acute level are only comfortable in the environment and setting, common to its belief system.

In reality the more spiritual we are the more easily we should be able to function in any social setting. For most Christians this setting is often referred to as the world. Ironically they are very happy with this label because it shows alignment with the statement that Jesus made that

'whosever is a friend of the world is an enemy of God.'

How sad that they fail to put into context all the words of Jesus. For example the above statement must be squared with what Jesus also said in *John 3v16.*

'For God so loved the world, that he lay down his life for it.'

Jesus was able to mix into any social setting. So much so that the religious people of His day called Him friend of sinners, prostitutes and publicans.

'He had no beauty or majesty to attract us to him, nothing in his appearance that we should desire him.'
Isaiah 53v2

The Scribes and Pharisees however stood out for all the wrong reasons.

'Everything they do is for men to see: They make their phylacteries wide and the tassels on their garments long; they love the place of honour at banquets and the most important seats in the synagogues; they love to be greeted in the market-place and to have men call them Rabbi.'
Matthew 23v5-7

People who are genuinely making good spiritual progress are at home in whatever environment, social or otherwise they find themselves in. They are at peace with themselves, their neighbour and the world around them. They function perfectly wherever they are.

CHAPTER 15

THE CHICKEN AND THE EGG SYNDROME

I once heard a lovely expression made by a friend of mine, who I considered to be a Godly man. He said about the established Christian Church:

> 'Its hard to find a Church that is not daft or dead, we major in the minors for most of the time'

Jesus said a similar thing about the established Church in His day

> "But you have neglected the more important matters of the law – justice, mercy and faithfulness. You should have practised the latter, without neglecting the former."
> Matthew 23v23

Most people have heard the saying

> "Give a man a fish, feed him for a day, teach a man how to fish and you feed him for life".[1]

Each of these expressions has at least one thing in common. Each asks the question which comes first?

Is discovering God first about Theology and then Reality or Reality then Theory? This question needs to be answered and answered urgently – "What is the priority?"

There is a wonderful book written by Steve Covey called 'First Things First'[2] – although the book is primarily aimed at businesses, its principles can be applied to all areas of life. In this book, the author opens up the understanding of how important it is to get priorities right.

Successful companies have long learned this valuable lesson and know how to prioritise jobs according to importance. Look at any person, group or organisation that is successful and amongst other things, you almost always see that they know how to prioritise.

I was stopped in my tracks while thinking about this chapter, by an item appearing on the 10pm BBC News programme. The item was about a new growing phenomenon in America that is called the 'Mega Church'. The news clip focussed on a Church in Texas pastored by Joel Osteen. The Church is growing so fast that it recently bought an ex baseball stadium to house a 30 thousand strong congregation, meeting every week. It is estimated that the number would rise to over 100 thousand within a few years.

In his commentary, the reporter said that a main aim of the Church was not to impose doctrinal truth, theology or even moral values, but rather to focus on meeting the practical needs of the people. Attendees who were interviewed, said that they felt that what was being taught was relevant and meaningful to their lives. As a result of the success of this Church, it was reported that the traditional Churches were closing at a rate of 60 per week.

Has this Church discovered the key to what its priority should be?

At this stage, it is hard to make any sweeping statements or come to any final conclusions. It is possible to present a 'sweet' attractive diet, that does not contain much substance, but has large appeal. Noticeable growth in all areas is paramount.

Look at the ministry of Jesus, He pushed passed dogma, creed and tradition and went out to meet the needs of the people. His first priority was to see to this aspect of people. *Matthew 15v32*[3]

Jesus gives us the priority:

> *"But seek first His Kingdom and His righteousness, and all these things will be given to you as well." Matthew 6v33*

Beyond any doubt, this was the cornerstone of His teachings. Note this carefully, if a man seeks first the Kingdom of God and His righteousness then everything else he has need of is provided. This is not an exaggeration, this is the only way to solve all the World's problems. There is no other way.

Let me be totally clear. The established Church tends to reverse this cornerstone instruction of Jesus, it prioritises theory above practical reality. It is more concerned that its members understand its interpretation of the Scripture. The starting point is simple. God, the Infinite one, the Creator, the Eternal Source, the Universe Spirit, (choose whichever word you are most comfortable with. There are many descriptions and names for God) is all Love, in Him there is no shadow of turning, there is no hidden agenda. He only wants to see love propagated throughout all eternity. Instruct people to search for Him and experience Him directly and they will find Him. Do not primarily concern yourself about your understanding or point of view or theology.

When people have found Him (God) for themselves, they will have correct theology. The day is coming when none will require a teacher.

> *"No longer will a man teach his neighbour, or a man his brother, saying 'Know the Lord,' because they will all know me, from the least of them to the greatest."*
> *Hebrews 8v11*

No way is this priority better stated than in the parable of the 'Good Samaritan.' *Luke 10v25-37*

The countrymen of the man who fell amongst thieves were more interested in etiquette and tradition, they were more concerned what others might think, and more concerned about themselves than to attend the needs of the wounded man. Along comes the 'Samaritan', who, from a traditional standpoint would have been regarded as an enemy of the Jews[4]. However, moved with compassion, he set about in a practical way to help. In conclusion of this parable, Jesus asks the question, *'who behaved like the neighbour to the Jewish man who had been beaten and left for dead?'*

Unless the Church learns how to reach over the traditional barriers of religion, we will never understand the ministry of Jesus. The words of the Church will seem (as to many already) irrelevant and out of date. I should also add that this need extends to all the major faiths. If individuals, the Church, religious organisations and the world do not learn how to do this, we will appear to be like Nero, who fiddled while Rome burned[5].

Summing up the parable of the Good Samaritan Jesus gives two commandments that we need to observe as our first priority:

(a)   Love the Lord your God with all your heart

(b)   Love your neighbour as yourself

If each person, every group, every Church and every nation worked on these qualities daily, the change in the world would be phenomenal. If we apply these two criteria to every decision we make, we are on the way to seeing the 'salvation' of the whole World.

CHAPTER 16

WHAT CAUSES WAR?

(The making of a terrorist)

Every Christian and Bible student should know the answer to this
question! The answer is given in black and white terms in *James 4v1-3*

> *"What causes fights and quarrels among you? Don't they
> come from your desires that battle within you? You want
> something but don't get it. You kill and covet, but you
> cannot have what you want. You quarrel and fight.
> You do not have, because you do not ask God. When you
> do not receive because you ask with wrong motives; that
> you may spend what you get on your pleasures"*

It seems to me that this is a picture of inner turmoil and confusion.
James gives us a clear picture here of how confused we really are inside
ourselves. On the one hand we are so unsure inside we don't know
what we want so don't know how to ask and at the same time, on the
other hand, when we get what we thought we wanted we soon realise it
is not actually what we want. I am sure this is very clear! (I don't think
this is what is meant by the expression 'don't let the right hand know
what the left one is doing').

How many times have you heard yourself arguing with passion some point of view, but deep down in yourself you know that you are not completely sure of your ground? Until we sort ourselves out, until our understanding (theory) matches up with our experience (reality) let us proceed with caution in how and what we do.

Inner turmoil is caused by unresolved questions inside ourselves.

When we begin life there is no turmoil, we are enveloped in the comfort of warmth and innocence. As we grow and become more aware of our surroundings the questions begin in earnest. Unfortunately the many and conflicting answers we receive often only serve to move us deeper into a fog of confusion and uncertainty.

It cannot be underestimated how much the first formative years of our lives affect nearly everything else we ever do. These formative years of our life are also known as the period when we are most impressionable.

There is therefore, tremendous responsibility on parents, teachers, and the community at large to see that the impression we give to children is of the highest quality emotionally, psychologically, morally and every other way which we can think of. No wonder Jesus warns

'It would be better for him to be thrown into the sea with a millstone tied round his neck than for him to cause one of these little ones to sin." Luke 17v2.

I have often looked on with great dismay whenever I see protest marches where parents have involved young children. They are made to carry banners with slogans they almost certainly don't understand the meaning of. They are often encouraged to join in shouting out chants they can barely pronounce. What effect is this having on young impressionable minds? I am even more concerned when these protests are political or religious in nature.

When we involve our young children in these sorts of activities we fuel the fire of hate, turmoil and war for the next generation to come. (I am not saying we should not teach our children how we see things, but we need to take care not to pass on our bias and prejudice). We need to find a better way. Ironically the way is for adults to become as little children!

> *'And he said: "I tell you the truth, unless you change and become like little children, you will never enter the kingdom of heaven." Matthew 18v3*

If only we can all get back to the state of innocence, where there is no conflict and turmoil. Becoming 'child-like' (not childish) is not as hard as it may first seem. All that is required is, for us to take a step back and ask the question,

"What do <u>I actually believe</u> about this situation?"

If we follow this question with total honesty, suspending judgement until we are totally convinced in our heart, we would soon arrive.

As I searched out answers to questions that I found confusing I began to experience a remarkable thing; I noticed I was 'unlearning' many things I had taken on board as 'gospel' that had no substance and foundation.

'Unlearning is part of Learning.' Steve Bryan

It is important to note that unlearning does not necessarily mean that what we currently know is wrong. However, it does mean that to move forward we have to let go one truth to reach after the next truth. Climbing a ladder would be a good example of this, every rung is necessary but you cannot reach the top without letting go of the lower rungs first.

I am no longer afraid to step aside from arguments and debates that are going nowhere. I say going nowhere, this is actually not strictly correct. They lead to divisions and feelings of ill will:

> *"Don't have anything to do with foolish and stupid arguments, because you know they produce quarrels." 2 Timothy 2v23.*

In the King James translation the word unlearned replaces the word stupid. This hits the truth of what is trying to be conveyed here more firmly on the head. Many times we argue a point we don't fully understand from the point of ignorance.

So how do we get to the terrorist?

Young impressionable minds that are subject to constant fundamentalist teaching, indoctrination and extremism are good candidates. The error is compounded when these young people are not allowed personal reflection or to challenge what they are being taught. Their view of the world becomes distorted. This scenario is currently the subject of endless debate here in the UK, particularly after the bombings on the London transport system.

Can a terrorist change?

Earlier in Chapter 3 I suggested that different groups within the Church were a result of the type of soil they were planted in. I could also have said that we reap what we sow. *Galatians 6v7-9.* If we indoctrinate our congregations or those that we lead with idealistic personal interpretations we are not far from producing a terrorist!

I believe that there is only one thing more dangerous than a fanatic. And that is a religious fanatic. A fanatic could be described as a person who can only see his or her point of view. When religious fervour is added to this type of emerging personality and character an explosive cocktail is produced. Everything a religious fanatic does is driven by a belief that he acts on God's behalf. Seeing that everyone conforms to 'Will of God' is a noble calling of which martyrdom is a price worth paying. Please note I am not calling all martyrs religious fanatics – follow the spirit and not the letter of what I am saying.

Well, let's look at one of the best biblical examples of someone who we would perhaps label as a terrorist if alive today. I refer to Saul who was so transformed that he became regarded as one of the greatest Apostles of all time.

When we first meet Saul in Acts 8 he had just presided over the murder of Stephen who was regarded as the first martyr of the Christian Church. Buoyed up by this he begins to make havoc within the Church *(Acts 8v3-4)*.

If we look carefully at his upbringing we see that as a young man he was heavily indoctrinated by his peers *(Acts 22v3)* and *Philippians 3v4-6.*

With Saul, as with others who have been heavily indoctrinated, it takes a radical step to bring about real change. At first there seems no reason why Saul should have such a dramatic 'conversion'. I have heard many say that if every one had such a blinding revelation we would all change. Saul's conversion was more miraculous than the norm we generally hear reported. However, 'God is no respecter of persons' He does not give one person preference or favours over another. We need to look more closely at his Damascus road conversion.

God makes the statement to Saul,

> *"..It is hard for thee to kick against the pricks.."* Acts *9v5*

Colloquially speaking God is saying to Saul

'it is hard for you to go against your conscience'

In other words on the surface of Saul's life he was going on with following the fundamental teaching he had received, but deep down inside he had a lot of unanswered questions. I think that these questions were deeply intensified when he saw the lives and response of those he was persecuting and killing. Instead of retaliating they responded with love. The questions grew to a level where an answer had to be forthcoming. Praise be to the living God. If we come to Him and ask Him what to believe His response is always as dramatic as it was for Saul. Change can always take place.

When relatives of victims of terrorist attacks and atrocities are asked how they feel, answers of bitterness, hatred and the call for revenge is often heard. However, I am sometimes very heartened on hearing the answers of others that talk about forgiveness and love. We will not overcome the terrorist with the sword! Love is the only answer.

When will fights and warring cease? When we stop pushing and insisting on our point of view. When we get on with the practical side of loving God and our neighbour as ourselves. You may not think that we are guilty of such things today; we need to take a closer clear look at ourselves.

Do you feel a 'knot' rising in your stomach when you hear a view expressed, not in keeping with your own? No matter how much you try to 'keep calm' you feel the 'righteous' anger building in yourself, particularly when the matter is on some point, you consider key, is challenged or contested. Out of a desire to 'correct' the error, we launch into debate and discussion that quickly deteriorates and spirals downwards.

Truth does not need you or I to defend it or prove it, no more than a circle needs to prove itself not a straight line!

CHAPTER 17

THE BLIND LEADING THE BLIND

What happens when *'the blind lead the blind?'* Jesus poses and answers this question *'they will both fall into a pit.' Matthew 15v12-14.*

To one degree or another, I believe that this has been going on at a global scale in every generation. It happens whenever an individual, a group of people, any organization, government etc., seeks to impose its will on any other. The problem is compounded when those imposing their will have no real root of certainty that their will and understanding is correct. It is compounded even more when those imposing their will believe that they alone are correct.

This book is an attempt to open our eyes to this reality so that we can break free of what has become a repeating cycle of events. Happily there are many that see what is happening and are working tirelessly to bring about changes that set people really free. When people are really free they are allowed to think for themselves without fear, they are allowed to pursue their true destiny and develop their real potential. They are even allowed to make and learn from their own mistakes!

The incident involving a man born blind as told in *John 9* brings together the various points I have been trying to illustrate in this book.

In summary then let's take a look at events surrounding this blind man and Jesus.

To aid the flow of these events I will outline the story and make the comparisons in square angle brackets with a change in typeface i.e. [comment]

The Story begins when the disciples of Jesus see the blind man and ask Him *'Who sinned, this man or his parents.'* It was a popular held belief that if someone had an affliction it was the result of their own sin or punishment to the parents for something they had done. In a way this was not an unreasonable belief to hold as the God of the Old Testament made the clear statement that He would do just that. *Exodus 20:5-6; 34:6-7; Numbers 14:18*

[There are grounds for old ways of thinking. Note Jesus does not contradict the Old Testament teaching]

Jesus makes the clear reply that neither reason is correct. What is more amazing He says the reason is so that God can make a point clear! *v3-5.*

[You cannot always assume that traditional thinking applies to all situations. God knows that making these kinds of changes requires dramatic illustrations. Implied here is letting a lower rung go to reach after a higher one]

Jesus then goes ahead and heals him and sends him home. When his friends and family see him, confusion breaks out. Some argue away the miracle by saying he just looks like the blind man, while others know its him but cannot explain how he can now see. The blind man himself can only describe the events that led up to him being able to see but cannot explain how he can now see. *V6-12.*

[Whenever God touches a person in a new way the initial response is often one of confusion. Not only are people around the one touched confused but the person themselves often have no answers. It is not that God wishes to confuse us but that change in thinking is always a radical action and needs time to be taken on board. For a while the picture appears more muddied than clearer.]

The debate then moves from friends and family to the Church authorities of the day. The authorities are not so much taken up with the miracle of the blind man now being able to see but are outraged that Jesus appears to have broken traditional law by doing work (healing) on a Saturday (Holy day). They argue that if He were a good man He would not have broken the law of the Sabbath.

[Now it really gets rough. This is what everyone who wants to think outside the box will experience. If following your heart takes you outside of what are traditional, historic, fundamental lines of belief expect strong opposition. Note here again the authorities are following Old Testament law and interpretation but only as they see it. They are not open to new possibilities.]

The authorities seeing the crowds divided ask the blind man for his account of events. The blind man concludes he must be a prophet. This angers the authorities even more who suspect this is some kind of hoax and call the blind man's parents to confirm his identity. Word has got around from the authorities that if anybody sides with Jesus they would be excommunicated from the Church. As a result of this the parents are intimidated. They acknowledge that this is their son who was born blind but now sees, but they do not want to get involved in understanding how the change took place. *V17-23*

[In this Duel we have to combat friends, relatives and even ourselves. We can expect threats and intimidations to make sure we tow the expected line. Reading this sort of account from a distance it is easy to miss the magnitude of what it means for those involved. Try and enter this story from each perspective and feel the situation.]

The authorities realising they are not winning the argument make one last attempt to get this blind man to see reason and their point of view. He gets another chance to back up their position. However, the blind man is not afraid to follow his own heart. By his own reasoning he works out that although he does not know who Jesus is He must be a good man. His reasoning is so powerful that the authorities are affronted that this ignorant man should attempt to teach them. They respond by throwing him out. *V24-34.*

[People who stand on the side of tradition, history, popular thinking and fundamentalism nearly always go back to playing their Ace card of bully when they are losing the argument. When people accuse you of not knowing what you are talking about, be encouraged, you are almost certainly on the right road.]

When the once blind man is thrown out of the Church Jesus comes and visits him. In the conversation with Jesus the man realises for the first time the significance of Jesus and his experience. Everything becomes crystal clear.

[We must walk through all the opposition when we follow our hearts. It is only as we emerge from the mist and fog, that all will become clear to our understanding. In other words clear understanding (theory) follows practical application. It is usually never the other way around. Notice that God always comes to us if we remain honest and open.]

Jesus' final words to those in authority was that while they remain closed to new possibilities they will remain blind leaders of the blind. Such people are best left to themselves.

[From experience you cannot help someone who does not

want to be helped. No one has the right to violate the freewill of another. Even being right does not give us this authority! This is a hallmark that you are on the right road.]

If I and you, our generation fight this good fight with all our might, we face this duel and win, then coming generations will not have to fight the same way. Theory will be done away with. We will provide a working practical model for our offspring to follow.

I have tried to show that putting theory first puts a stumbling block in the way of the evolution of mankind on his journey back to God – in fact, puts it in reverse! Practical theory opens the way straight to God Himself, who is all loving, all faith and all joy. It is the sincere desire of my heart that this God *in him we live and move and have our being, Acts 17v22-31*, might be felt and known by all men everywhere. '*To the only God, our Saviour be glory, majesty, power and authority through Jesus Christ our Lord, before all ages, now and for evermore! Amen.' Jude 24-25*

This is the message that our generation must learn, or we must continue to wander more years in the wilderness, around the same mountain. *Deuteronomy 8v2.*

This book is not about new theology, it does not seek to challenge your theology or basis of faith. It purely seeks to put first things first. Get the love right and the theology will take care of itself. Allow people to grow in God and they will grow in love. Our God is infinite and expresses Himself infinitely through diversities.

> "You have heard that it was said, 'Eye for eye, and tooth for tooth.' But I tell you, Do not resist an evil person. If someone strikes you on the right cheek, turn to him the other also. And if someone wants to sue you and take your tunic, let him have your cloak as well. If someone forces you to go one mile, go with him two miles. Give to the one who asks you, and do not turn away from the one who wants to borrow from you.

You have heard that it was said, 'Love your neighbour and hate your enemy.' But I tell you: Love your enemies and pray for those who persecute you, that you may be sons of your Father in heaven. He causes his sun to rise on the evil and the good, and sends rain on the righteous and the unrighteous. If you love those who love you, what reward will you get? Are not even the tax collectors doing that? And if you greet only your brothers, what are you doing more than others? Do not even pagans do that?" - (Matthew 5:38-47)

CHAPTER 18

THE ANSWER IS LOVE

In any duel there is not only the possibility of winning but also the possibility of losing or even being killed.

Everything hinges on the outcome.

For most people the ultimate fear of dying can be paralysing. In the context of this book this is seen as error caused either by thinking outside the box or as rejection of our point of view by our peers.

We would all be a lot more relaxed about life if we could take away the fear of dying from the equation of the duel.

If you and I could see and know for certain that death is only an illusion, with no real substance, our attitude would change immediately. Moreover if the whole world could grasp this truth we would begin to really live at peace with our neighbours. We would have a solid basis on which we could do away with weapons and nuclear deterrents. The world would readily *'beat their swords into ploughshares and their spears into pruning hooks'. Micah 4v3*

To see and know for certain that death is only an illusion is both hard and easy. This is probably the ultimate paradox of life. It is hard in that the fear of dying is the last enemy that will be overcome. *1 Corinthians 15v26.* Easy in the sense that perfect love drives out all fear, *1 John 4v18,* even the fear of dying.

In short love is the answer.

Although unravelling this paradox requires real effort on the part of each person, the love can be readily gained by every person living on the planet without exception.

The love talked of here is not sentimental, mushy or even physical in nature. It has little to do with what most of us call 'family' love either. The Greeks have 4 words for love. The type of love spoken of here is the one referred to as *Agape* love. It is unconditional love flowing from the very heart of God. It is the love that is spoken of in *John 15v13*

> *"Greater love has no-one than this, that he lay down his life for his friends."*

This Agape Love is the <u>greatest</u> force in the whole of the universe and therefore cannot be overcome.

To achieve this love we must allow it to grow in our hearts. To allow it to grow we must spend more time in the presence of God Himself who is by definition love *1 John 4:16-21*. In Christian terminology this is the process of meditation and contemplation. When we spend time in God's presence it is the same as spending time sunbathing on the beach. This very act exposes us to its rays and without our interference our skin is tanned as a result of this exposure. Joyfully there are no downside effects of the rays of love that bathe us when we come into the presence of God!

With love as the answer we can follow our hearts without fear of death in this duel. If our point of view is rejected or we are criticised or made to suffer in any way because we think outside of the box, we can know for certain that all will be well. We gain both strength and patience to go where God leads us. It takes the weapons from the hands of those who seek to tie us in tradition and history. It takes away the power from those who indoctrinate and poison the lives of vulnerable, growing young people who wittingly or unwittingly seek to turn them into copies of themselves.

If you are a leader of any description or in any area, do you lead by love or by fear and intimidation? Do you threaten those that you lead seeking to bring them into line by fear? If so you need to stop and examine your own heart. This is not the way of love.

The way of love offers to *'turn the other cheek' Matthew 5:38:45.* when its views are pushed to the side. We have to find this out practically for ourselves. Theory on this point will not help at all.

1 Corinthians chapter 13 gives us the best definition the world has ever had of what Love really is:

> *"If I speak in the tongues of men and of angels, but have not love, I am only a resounding gong or a clanging cymbal.*
>
> *If I have the gift of prophecy, and fathom all mysteries, and all knowledge, and I have a faith that can move mountains, but have not love, I am nothing.*
>
> *If I give all I possess to the poor, and surrender my body to the flames, but have not love, I gain nothing.*
>
> *Love is patient, love is kind. It does not envy, it does not boast, it is not proud. It is not rude, it is not self-seeking, it is not easily angered, it keeps no record of wrongs. Love does not delight in evil but rejoices with the truth. It always protects, always trusts, always hopes, always perseveres.*

Love never fails. But where there are prophecies, they will cease; where there are tongues, they will be stilled; where there is knowledge, it will pass away. For we know in part and we prophesy in part, but when perfection comes, the imperfect disappears. When I was a child, I talked like a child, I thought like a child, I reasoned like a child. When I became a man, I put childish ways behind me. Now we see but a poor reflection as in a mirror; then we shall see face to face. Now I know in part; then I shall know fully, even as I am fully known.

And now these three remain: faith, hope and love. But the greatest of these is love."

The 'Ex terrorist' Paul states

"For I am convinced that neither death nor life, neither angels nor demons, neither the present nor the future, nor any powers, neither height nor depth, nor anything else in all creation, will be able to separate us from the LOVE OF GOD that is in Christ Jesus our Lord."

Romans 8v38-39

Dear Reader

The sum total of all of this is simple:

Love God with all your heart, with all your might, with all your soul and love your neighbour as yourself.

Follow these two commands, then follow your heart wherever it takes you. With this simple formula you cannot fail, you free yourself and those around you. You will find new heights and joys that we can only dream of at this time.

Epilogue

'The Duel' is a request that we all pause for a moment and stop fighting each other. Instead we should fight and wrestle with ourselves. By ourselves I mean our conscience. What is this conscience but our own personal higher voice, it is the messenger of God, His angel sent to protect us.

When Jacob wrestled with his angel all night, and prevailed, he was rewarded by seeing Heaven opened up to him. Shortly afterwards, he found that his brother had not come to fight him but rather to be reconciled. [1]

If we wrestle with our angel and prevail, then like Jacob Heaven will be opened up to us as well. We will be reconciled to our brother, neighbour and those of other faith and practices. We will not see an enemy but only another side of ourselves.

There is a real place that every human being can come to regardless of religion, background or culture.

It is a real place where you can be at peace with God, the World and yourself.

It is a real place that can only be experienced. You cannot enter it by intellectual debate or any amount of learning.

It is a real place that will transform what seems idealistic in this book, to absolute reality.

In this book there are enough clues to arrive at this real place.

Those who seek earnestly <u>will</u> find it!

www.the-duel.info

APPENDIX

<u>Preface</u>

All quotes are from the NIV Bible, unless otherwise stated.

<u>A message to you</u>

1. From a sermon by the English author John Downe

<u>Chapter 1</u>

1. As well as appearing on Korean television, the Choirs have sung all over the world and produced a variety of CD's. (Information taken from the programme)
2. Grammy-award winning Larnelle Harris, is based in Kentucky USA and sang his first concert at the age of nine. He has two children, a boy and girl, and enjoys his music ministry all over the world. He has composed over 30 songs and produced over 18 albums. (Information taken from the programme)
3. I Robot, 2004 Twentieth Century Fox Film Corporation.

<u>Chapter 2</u>

1. In using the word solitary it does not necessarily mean we withdraw to a place of isolation – although for some it may mean just that. In general I use the term to mean detached in an inward sense.

<u>Chapter 3</u>

1. Official Biography by Jamie Buckingham, Bridge-Logos Publishers; Commemorate edition (August 1, 1999)
2. Smith Wigglesworth: The Complete Collection of His Life Teachings, Harrison House (March 1, 1997)
3. The Collected Works of Saint John of the Cross by St John of the Cross, Kieran Kavanaugh, I C S Publications, Institute of Carmelite St; Revised edition (January 1, 1991)

Chapter 4

1. If Magazine issue 23, Summer 2005. © 2005 Toyota (GB) PLC

Chapter 5

1. http://www.greatsite.com/timeline-english-bible-history/

Chapter 6

1. Source: http://en.wikipedia.org/wiki/trinity
2. From The Seven Ecumenical Councils, ed. H. Percival, in the Library of Nicene and Post Nicene Fathers, 2nd series (New York: Charles Scribners, 1990), Vol XIV, 3
3. From Discover the Power Within You by Eric Butterworth. ISBN 0-06-250115-1

Chapter 8

1. Modern History Sourcebook: The Crime of Galileo: Indictment and Abjuration of 1633
2. http://www.channel4.com/entertainment/tv/microsites/S/spacecadets/
3. The Truman Show is a movie made in 1998 directed by Peter Weir. It is the story about a character who escapes from an environment of media illusions.
4. Space Cowboys is a 2000 film by Clint Eastwood, released by Warner Bros., about four aged ex-astronauts who are sent into space to repair an old satellite.
5. The Matrix, a film released in 1999 written and directed by Larry and Andy Wachowski. Everyday life is turned upside-down when Thomas Anderson discovers that the world around him is a detailed virtual reality created by a computer that has taken over the Earth of the future. When Anderson realizes his predicament he teams up with Morpheus, the leader of a gang of freedom fighters, to reclaim their individuality and 'wake up' the world. (From Cinescape.)

Chapter 9

1. The Seven Spiritual Laws of Success by Deepak Chopra, New World Library (January 1, 1995)

2. Said in an interview on Thursday 28th July 2005 Radio 4 Today programme. (Sadly, since writing this book, Lord Donaldson has passed away.)

Chapter 10

1. Discover the Power Within by Eric Butterworth, HarperSanFrancisco First Published 1968 Last reprinted August 14, 1992 Page 32
2. How to Know God by Deepak Chopra, Three Rivers Press (February 20, 2001)

Chapter 11

1. http://www.guardian.co.uk/commentisfree/story/0,,1944243,00.html

Chapter 15

1. Chinese proverb, author unknown.
2. First Things First by Stephen R. Covey, A. Roger Merrill and Rebecca R. Merrill, Simon & Schuster Ltd, 1994
3. Mathew 15v32. Jesus called his disciples to him and said, "I have compassion for these people; they have already been with me."
4. John 4v9. The Jews had no dealings with the Samaritans. The Jews regarded all Samaritans as 'unclean'.
5. Emperor Nero Claudius Caesar couldn't have fiddled while Rome burned in A.D. 64 because the violin wasn't invented until the 1500s. What Nero really did while Rome burned is sing. The Emperor, who had artistic ambitions, was apparently performing an old Greek scene for his friends. The reference to fiddle was to engage in frivolous activity.

Epilogue

1. Genesis 28v10-17, Genesis 32 & 33

Printed in the United Kingdom
by Lightning Source UK Ltd.
123303UK00002B/1-99/A